The Psycholo
Job Interview

Most people, at some point in their lives, experience the stress of being interviewed for a job. Many also face the task of interviewing other people. But what does the science tell us about this unique social situation? What biases are involved, and how can we become aware of them? And how can job interviews be structured so that they are fair and effective?

This second edition of *The Psychology of Job Interviews* provides an accessible and concise overview of what we know. Based on empirical research rather than secondhand advice, it discusses the strategies and tactics that both applicants and interviewers can use to make their interviews more successful; from how to make a good first impression to how to decide which candidate is the best fit for the role. Updated throughout, this timely new edition comes with an additional chapter focused on technology in interviewing. Also featuring the addition of a new "Toolbox" at the end of chapters with practical summaries, tools, advice, and concrete examples, the book guides job applicants on how best to prepare for and perform in an interview and provides managers with best-practice advice in selecting the right candidate.

Debunking several popular myths along the way, this is essential reading for anyone interested in understanding what is really happening in a job interview, whichever side of the desk you are sitting.

Dr. Nicolas Roulin is Associate Professor of Industrial/Organizational Psychology at Saint Mary's University in Halifax, Canada. He is an expert in personnel selection and his work has been published in top psychology and management journals. He has worked with assessment companies in Canada and internationally.

The Psychology of Job Interviews

Second Edition

Dr. Nicolas Roulin

Routledge
Taylor & Francis Group

LONDON AND NEW YORK

Cover image: © Getty Images

Second edition published 2022
by Routledge
4 Park Square, Milton Park, Abingdon, Oxon, OX14 4RN

and by Routledge
605 Third Avenue, New York, NY 10158

Routledge is an imprint of the Taylor & Francis Group, an informa business

First edition published by Routledge 2017

British Library Cataloguing-in-Publication Data
A catalogue record for this book is available from the British Library

Library of Congress Cataloging-in-Publication Data
Names: Roulin, Nicolas, author.
Title: The psychology of job interviews / Dr. Nicolas Roulin.
Description: Second edition. | Abingdon, Oxon ; New York, NY :
    Routledge, 2022. | Includes bibliographical references and index.
Identifiers: LCCN 2021036316 (print) | LCCN 2021036317 (ebook) |
    ISBN 9780367773786 (paperback) | ISBN 9780367773793 (hardback) |
    ISBN 9781003171089 (ebook)
Subjects: LCSH: Employment interviewing—Psychological aspects. |
    Personnel management—Psychological aspects. | Psychology, Industrial.
Classification: LCC HF5549.5.I6 R68 2022 (print) | LCC HF5549.5.I6
    (ebook) | DDC 650.14/4019—dc23
LC record available at https://lccn.loc.gov/2021036316
LC ebook record available at https://lccn.loc.gov/2021036317

ISBN: 978-0-367-77379-3 (hbk)
ISBN: 978-0-367-77378-6 (pbk)
ISBN: 978-1-003-17108-9 (ebk)

DOI: 10.4324/9781003171089

Typeset in Bembo
by Apex CoVantage, LLC

Contents

What is a job interview and why do organizations use it?

The role of a job interview when selecting employees

Rachel and Kareem just graduated from the same university with a degree in mechanical engineering. They are ready to enter the labour market and start their quest for the ideal job. They both have identified a handful of organizations that have a good reputation and are looking for engineers with backgrounds like theirs. But it is their first time applying for "real" jobs. What will the hiring process look like for them? Here is a snapshot of what they might be expected to face.

Initially, Rachel and Kareem will be asked to formally apply to each position (most likely online) and provide information that will allow the hiring organization to engage in an initial screening procedure. With many online applications, this might also involve completing a standardized form including information about their education, work experience, or availabilities. They may also be asked to send or upload a resume, a cover letter, proofs of their education credentials, and perhaps a list of references. This initial screening stage has two objectives. First, before investing time and resources in assessing candidates, the organization wants to ensure that applicants like Rachel and Kareem possess the basic qualifications to perform the

DOI: 10.4324/9781003171089-1

job. Second, if they apply for the same position, Rachel and Kareem will compete against each other and likely other job applicants for the same position (or positions). If the ratio of the number of applicants to the number of jobs available is quite large, the organization may not have the resources to assess all applicants in depth. It thus has to make quick screening decisions based on limited information in order to eliminate the least qualified candidates and focus only on a smaller pool of promising individuals.

If Rachel and Kareem pass this first hurdle, they may be asked (on some occasions) to complete tests to further assess personal characteristics that the organization deems important for joining their team. This can include assessments of cognitive abilities, personality traits, workstyle preferences, integrity, or values. But what is usually at the core of the selection process is the job interview. Surveys conducted around the world are unanimous: most organizations include some form of job interview as part of their hiring process.[1] It is therefore very unlikely that Rachel or Kareem will ever get a job offer before interviewing with one or several representatives from the hiring organization (in some cases using technology, as described in Chapter 5).

As we will see in more detail later, interviews can take multiple forms, can be more or less effective at identifying the best candidate for the position, and can leave positive or negative memories for those who have experienced them. Yet, independently of all this, the job interview always has a special status for organizations. It is a gate through which almost all job applicants have to pass before they become organization members. The interviewer (or interviewers, in some cases) is the gatekeeper, whose role is to verify that the applicant is worthy before they can enter. In other words, if the organization is a high-end nightclub, the interviewer is the bouncer deciding if party-seekers at the door correspond to the profile of clients that the club wants. Despite the important role of job interviews, both applicants and interviewers are often non-experts who enter the interview room with mixed feelings. They understand the importance of this encounter for their future (or the future of their team, department, or organization) and thus want to demonstrate professionalism, impress their interaction partner, and make optimal decisions. At the same time, they may be uncertain about what to expect from the interview, experience anxiety about how to behave, and worry about making mistakes.

The goal of this book is to present an overview of the job interview that can be useful to a variety of audiences that have an interest in interviews: applicants currently on the job market, professional Human Resource (HR) managers, managers who are not HR experts but have to act as interviewers to select future employees, or psychology and management students who want to understand how interviews really work. Unlike the majority of interview-related books available on the market, the present text is not a "how-to" guide designed to help applicants "beat" the system with rehearsed answers to popular interview questions. It can, nevertheless, be helpful to better understand what could be expected from an interview, how to best prepare for it, and what strategies or behaviours can help increase the chances of obtaining a job offer. It is also not a book written by a management *guru* or seasoned interviewer describing their view on the best interviewing techniques based personal experiences (although I have experience interviewing applicants and helping organizations design interviews). Rather, it is a summary of the accumulated evidence about job interviews based on decades of theoretical and empirical research performed by psychology and management scholars from all around the world.

Throughout this book, I will present scientific facts about the psychology of job interviews. Some of those facts may appear intuitive to the reader, whereas others may contradict popular beliefs or personal experiences, and hopefully the book will encourage readers to rethink some of their interviewing practices. Although I may use some technical concepts here and there, I will refrain from using scientific jargon or from reporting some of the complex statistical analyses behind my arguments. However, I provide the reader with references to some key academic articles should they wish to pursue such enriching (yet possibly difficult) additional readings. I also illustrate these facts with numerous examples and practical recommendations, which will help job applicants to successfully prepare for interviews and help interviewers to conduct interviews and make optimal selection decisions. For instance, throughout the book we will follow our two fictitious applicants, Rachel and Kareem, in their experiences as applicants interviewing for various positions. We will also see what happens (or could happen) on the other side of the table with interviewers from various organizations (fictive ones, although mostly based on real cases).

The pursuit of "fit" between applicants and organizations

The job interview sometimes has the reputation of being similar to a police interrogation, in which the applicant is seen as a suspect and the interviewer is portrayed as an investigator trying to uncover evidence of problems associated with past work experiences. I do not pretend that interviewers never act as police investigators (some of them do!), nor do I suggest that applicants never lie or hide things that may hurt their candidacy (they sometimes do, as I discuss in Chapter 4). However, I argue that this reputation is largely unwarranted. Most of the time, the job interview is simply a social interaction between two (or more) individuals who want to exchange information or send signals about their qualities.[2]

Both applicants and interviewers send signals to each other. For job applicants, the interview is a platform to present their knowledge, skills, abilities, and past experiences or accomplishments, ideally aligning those qualities and successes with the position they are applying for or the organization's values. Similarly, interviewers use the interview to describe the features of the job; the team or department the applicant may be joining; or, more broadly, the values, mission, or objectives of the organization. In parallel to sending signals, applicants and interviewers also interpret and analyse the signals they receive. Applicants evaluate the information about the job to verify that it corresponds to their profile and meets their career ambitions. They also gauge the information about the team and organization to estimate whether they would enjoy working in such an environment. At the same time, interviewers assess whether the applicants' qualities correspond to what the organization is looking for.

On the applicants' side, the information collected and interpreted will be instrumental in making a decision on whether or not they want to pursue their application and eventually accept a job offer. On the interviewers' side, the goal is to decide who among the interviewees would be the best employee for the organization. Usually, interviewers do so by establishing two subjective indicators of "fit."[3] First, they estimate the level of person–job fit (or P-J fit). Interviewers thus evaluate if applicants possess the qualifications (e.g., education, skills, experience) that correspond to the job requirements – that is, whether they will be able to effectively perform the tasks and activities associated with the position. Second, they estimate the level of person-organization fit (or P-O fit). Interviewers thus evaluate whether an applicant's personality, values, or interests correspond to the team's or organization's values and culture – that is, whether they are likely to thrive in the organization and remain loyal employees.

Let's go back to Rachel and Kareem, our young job applicants. In each of the organizations in which they will interview, the interviewer (or interviewers) will ask them a series of questions. Ideally, these questions will provide them with opportunities to talk about things like who they are as individuals and what their qualities and qualifications are. Rachel and Kareem have received similar educations and hold the same engineering degree. Their technical skills and knowledge are thus relatively similar. Yet, they are very different people. They have different personalities. Rachel is very conscientious and hard-working, but she is an introvert when dealing with others. Kareem is much more extraverted, but he can sometimes jump too fast to conclusions when working on a task. They also have different "soft" skills. Despite her relative introversion, Rachel is a natural leader and great communicator. Kareem is a problem-solver and is very creative. Interviewers will use the information gathered during the interview to assess whether Rachel's and Kareem's qualities fulfil the requirements of the specific job they applied for (i.e., if there is a good P-J fit). They will also try to estimate if Rachel or Kareem as a person would be comfortable working in their unique work environment, and if their values and objectives correspond to those of the organization (i.e., if there is a good P-O fit). Interviewers will consider Rachel or Kareem for the position only if those two objectives are met (or, at least, if they are met to larger extent than when examining other candidates).

Assessments of P-J and P-O fit during a job interview are based on interviewers' perceptions and judgments, and thus they are subject to biases and decision errors. As I will discuss in the next chapters, there are ways for organizations and interviewers to reduce the subjectivity and biases associated with the interviewing process. However, it is important to understand that job interviews do not guarantee that the best hiring decision will be made all the time. They only allow organizations to predict the future success of an employee with some level of accuracy.

The prediction of future work behaviours and performance

One of the major objectives of all selection methods is to predict (as precisely as possible) the likelihood that an applicant, if offered a position, will behave in accordance with the organization's expectations and effectively perform job activities. This applies to all forms of assessments or tests used by organizations, including job interviews. Yet, it does not mean that interviewers will look into applicants' eyes and magically deduce what will happen in their future, like a wizard would do with a crystal ball. An interviewer is not a wizard and should not try to act like one! Taking the path of guesses or intuition-based decisions is dangerous. And, research clearly suggests that hiring decisions based on intuition or gut feeling are likely to be suboptimal, even when performed by seasoned interviewers.[4] Predictions in the context of selection should rather be interpreted as an uncertainty-reduction attempt to make an informed decision.

Last week, Rachel and Kareem both applied for an engineering position at a company called TopTech. Today, they both will be interviewed by Sonia, the local HR manager. To understand how Sonia's potential predictions work, let's take Kareem as the illustration here. Sonia does not know Kareem, and they never met before the interview. This means that, at the time of Kareem's application, Sonia had no prior information to assess his suitability for the job and to predict his future job performance. If she had to make a decision about hiring him (or not), this decision will be based on pure chance (equivalent to flipping a coin and hiring Kareem if the coin shows heads). Let's set such a chance-level decision as the "0" on our prediction scale. Let's now imagine a (very unrealistic) situation in which Sonia has the power to hire Kareem, jump five years into the future to see how he performed in the company since he was hired, and then come back to today. This situation would lead to a decision under perfect information (or no uncertainty) because Sonia "knows" what will happen to Kareem in the future. Let's set this as "100" on our prediction scale. Every piece of information that Sonia collects about Kareem during the selection process should help her to make a better prediction on our scale. Evaluating the information provided on Kareem's resume will already make Sonia's prediction higher than 0. Similarly, Kareem's answers in a job interview will help make this prediction rise more on our scale.

In personnel selection research, this prediction scale is called *predictive validity*. Scholars have accumulated evidence about the predictive validity of various selection methods.[5] Some methods have a relatively poor predictive validity. For instance, using graphology (i.e., analyzing someone's writing to assess personal character) is estimated to be around 2/100. Looking at the number of years of education only gives a predictive validity of 10/100. Some other methods have an average predictive validity, like a measure of the conscientiousness aspect of someone's personality (i.e., around 30/100). The best predictive validities are usually somewhere between 50/100 and 60/100 – for instance, with a cognitive ability test (e.g., an IQ test) or a work sample test (e.g., a brief activity that exactly simulates job activities, like a typing test for a secretary).

As you have probably noticed, even the best selection methods are still relatively far away from a perfect 100 score. Why? All those methods assess individual characteristics of the applicants. Although those characteristics can have an important impact on the performance of an employee at work, their performance will also depend on a multitude of unforeseeable external factors. Such factors may include the colleagues they work with, the quality of their direct supervisor, the existing procedures or rules in the organization, the reward and compensation systems in place, the economic context, changes in their health or familial situation, etc. Therefore, finding selection methods that have a predictive validity close to 100 is extremely unlikely. It is impossible to perfectly predict the future success of an applicant (at least not with the tools currently at our disposal). Similarly, even when organizations make hiring decisions based on a combination of selection tools (e.g., scores on a variety of tests or assessments), the combined validity will never approach 100.[6] This is because most assessment methods include some level of imprecision and rely on similar information about the applicant, so their predictive value cannot simply be summed up. As an example, if an organization uses a cognitive ability test (with a predictive validity of about 50/100) and a test of conscientiousness (with a predictive validity of about 30/100), the combined predictive validity is estimated to be around 60/100 (not 80/100).

This has two important implications that organizations and managers have to understand: (1) unfortunately, even the selection methods with the highest predictive validity will sometimes lead to *bad* hiring decisions; and (2) in the long run, the proportion of *good* hiring decisions will be much higher (and the proportion of *bad* decisions lower) when using valid (as compared to less valid) methods. In other words, relying on a well-designed and well-conducted (i.e., more valid) selection process will not protect organizations from making a few hiring mistakes, but it will guarantee a much larger number (or proportion) of optimal hiring decision over the course of multiple hires.

What makes interviews good predictors of future performance?

What about job interviews? There is not one clear predictive validity score for interviews, simply because interviews can be designed and conducted in very different ways. Unlike standardized tests, which are generally designed and administered in consistent ways following strict protocols, interviews can vary in length, type of questions asked, or approach to the evaluation of applicants' answers. As such, interviews can demonstrate very poor (i.e., as low as around 15/100) or very high (as high as 60/100) predictive validity.[7] In order words, a poorly designed and conducted interview will provide very little insight into the applicant's potential to perform in the organization. However, a well-designed interview conducted appropriately can be an excellent instrument to assess an applicant.

The characteristics of a well-designed and well-conducted job interview will be discussed in the next two chapters. Yet, it is important for the reader to understand the reasons why some interviews work better than others. Well-designed interviews are better predictors of job performance largely because they have higher *construct validity* and higher *reliability*. I will describe these two concepts and their importance below, and I will illustrate them with the example of Sonia interviewing Rachel and Kareem.

The construct validity of a job interview refers to the appropriateness of the job-related characteristics that one aims to assess via questions directed to the applicant.[8] In order words, are interviewers asking the appropriate questions? To ensure high construct validity, interviewers have to follow a series of steps when designing interview questions. First, they have to understand the specificities of the job they are hiring for and determine the knowledge, skills, abilities, or competencies necessary to perform that job. This step is usually relatively easy for line managers, who are experts in the job activities (because they perform the job themselves or supervise those performing it). However, this step can be daunting for HR specialists, who often hire for a large number of jobs and may not be very familiar with every single one of them. Second, interviewers have to translate those job requirements into interview questions, making sure that every key requirement will be properly evaluated by asking one or several questions. This task is usually complex for line managers, who sometimes can be unsure about the best way to formulate questions. This is why it is recommended that line managers and HR specialists work together to determine the job requirements and then translate them into interview questions.

How does it work in practice? Sonia, the HR manager, has to interview Rachel and Kareem (and likely other applicants) for a junior mechanical engineer position at TopTech. Sonia is not an engineer herself and therefore is unsure about the necessary skills or abilities for the position. She will get in touch with Danielle, the manager in charge of the engineering team. Sonia will ask Danielle about the key job activities and the qualities a good engineer must possess. If they want more precise information, Sonia and Danielle could also talk with engineers currently working in similar roles in the company, asking them about typical or particularly challenging aspects of their job and how they handle them. At the end of this process, Sonia and Danielle could agree, for example, that the ideal applicant must possess advanced knowledge in technology, physics, and maths; be a good communicator; and be able to think critically, analyse complex information, and solve difficult problems. They will then translate those qualities into interview questions – for instance, by designing a question that will assess communication, such as, "Tell me about a time when you had to explain something complex (for instance a complex concept, technical features, etc.) to someone who was not familiar with it. What was the complex issue and how did you proceed?" They will also make sure that all the key qualifications that the new hire must possess are assessed by at least one interview question.

The reliability of a job interview refers to level of consistency reached by multiple interviewers assessing the same applicant.[9] This means that two different interviewers conducting the same interview with the same applicant should reach similar conclusions about the applicant's suitability for the position. If they do not, this suggests that there is a problem with the way the interview was designed and/or conducted. Another way to understand the concept of reliability is to use the example of baking. Imagine that you are trying to bake delicious muffins together with a friend. One of the key tools necessary to perform this ambitious task is a weighing scale, which will help you to use the right quantity of flour or sugar. Imagine that you put a bowl on your scale and fill it with sugar until your scale indicates 200 grams (or about 7 oz.). Then you hand out the bowl to your friend and ask them to check the quantity again with the same scale. However, this time the scale indicates 255 grams (or about 8 oz.). You can ignore this problem and continue your preparation with a high risk that your muffins will end up not as delicious as you expected. Or, you can acknowledge that there is likely a problem with your tool, and you need to resolve it before moving on. In that case, changing the weighing scale may be the best solution.

The same thing applies to interviewing. Sonia and Danielle just finished two one-hour interviews with Rachel and Kareem, asking them a total of ten questions each. They agreed that each question would be worth up to ten points, for a total of 100. After the interview, they meet in Danielle's office to discuss their conclusions.

Box 1.1

Danielle starts the conversation: "I was really impressed by Kareem. I think he was probably the best candidate we have seen so far."

Sonia is shocked: "What?!? I think he was not bad, but certainly not our best candidate. Rachel did better, I think. I gave Kareem a total of 60/100 and Rachel 75/100. What about you?"

Danielle is apparently upset: "I gave Kareem 85/100 and Rachel 65/100. I would honestly hire him right now if I could. I gave him the maximum score for half of the questions. I think he could have done a bit better on a few others. But he was

continued . . .

---

cont.

really a nice and handsome guy. I can imagine him being my successor in a few years."

Sonia disagrees: "Maybe he is a nice guy, but he responded quite poorly on a few important questions, like the ones about communication and especially his motivation for the job. Rachel did much better on those questions."

Danielle is not convinced: "Again, I disagree. I gave him 9/10 for the motivation question. I think he was very knowledgeable about what we do in the company."

Sonia looks stunned: "Yes, he clearly knew what we manufacture here. But that was not what the question was about. It was supposed to assess how motivated he was to join us and stay here for the foreseeable future. I gave him a six. Rachel was much more convincing to me!"

In this example, there is a clear lack of consistency between Sonia's and Danielle's ratings. They obtain very different scores for Kareem (and Rachel) both for individual questions and in the total score. Their interview obviously lacks reliability. There can be multiple reasons for why this is the case. Most importantly, the scoring system is probably unclear. Although they have points to allocate, the way this is supposed to be done was likely not precisely defined and not standardized enough. This leads to situations where the same response from Kareem is interpreted in very different ways by Sonia and Danielle. For instance, Danielle allocates nine points for motivation, while Sonia gives only six points. It also appears that our two interviewers had different views of what some questions were designed to assess (which may also come from a lack of construct validity for those questions). Finally, Danielle's judgment may have been influenced by non-job-related factors, such as Kareem's handsome looks.

In summary, high-quality job interviews are those that are designed and conducted in ways that insure high *construct validity*, high *reliability*, and indirectly, high *predictive validity*. Such interviews have many advantages for organizations. Most importantly, they help assessing all job applicants in a consistent and efficient way, thus ensuring the highest likelihood of hiring the best job applicants. They also limit potential biases and judgment errors that could put an organization at risk, for instance if it is sued by a rejected applicant who believes that a decision was unfair (or violated local employment laws).

Overview of the remaining chapters

In the next chapters, I will present ways to design (Chapter 2) and conduct (Chapter 3) job interviews that limit some of the problems highlighted above, and thus improve the reliability, the construct validity, and indirectly the predictive validity of job interviews. I will also describe how job applicants react to selection decisions and what can be done to limit negative reactions from not-selected applicants. From the candidate's standpoint, these initial chapters explain what organizations are trying to assess by asking different types of questions and what can be done to best anticipate them. I will then describe the strategies and tactics that applicants can use to influence interviewers' evaluations and the ways interviewers attempt to convince applicants that they should join the organization (Chapter 4). Next, I describe some of the most important ways to integrate technology into the interviewing process (Chapter 5) as well as how technology impacts candidates' experiences and changes managers' roles. I also discuss the decision phase of the interview (Chapter 6), which highlights potential biases and errors that interviewers can make as well as considers how to avoid them (or at least limit their impact). Finally, I conclude with an overview of recent and future trends for job interviews, notably the potential role of equity, diversity, and inclusion initiatives (Chapter 7). Throughout this book, I also describe cultural and legal difference that may impact the appropriateness of interviewing techniques in different regions or countries. Although the majority of interview-related research to date has been conducted in North America and Western Europe, I will also describe and incorporate existing evidence of interviewing (or, more generally, managerial) practices from other regions of the world. At the end of each chapter, I include a "Toolbox," which provides specific tips, recommendations, or examples that the reader can use in their applications or interviews.

Notes

1   Steiner, D.D., *Personnel selection across the globe*, in *The Oxford Handbook of Personnel Assessment and Selection*, N. Schmitt, Editor. 2012, Oxford University Press: New York. p. 740–767.

2   Bangerter, A., N. Roulin, and C.J. König, *Personnel selection as a signaling game*. Journal of Applied Psychology, 2012. **97**(4): p. 719–738.

3   Kristof-Brown, A.L., *Perceived applicant fit: Distinguishing between recruiters' perceptions of person-job and person-organization fit*. Personnel Psychology, 2000. **53**(3): p. 643–671.

4   Highhouse, S., *Stubborn reliance on intuition and subjectivity in employee selection*. Industrial and Organizational Psychology, 2008. **1**(3): p. 333–342.

5   Schmidt, F.L. and J.E. Hunter, *The validity and utility of selection methods in personnel psychology: Practical and theoretical implications of 85 years of research findings*. Psychological Bulletin, 1998. **124**: p. 262–274.

6   Sackett, P.R., et al., *Effects of predictor weighting methods on incremental validity*. Journal of Applied Psychology, 2017. **102**(10): p. 1421–1434.

7   Campion, M.A., D.K. Palmer, and J.E. Campion, *A review of structure in the selection interview*. Personnel Psychology, 1997. **50**: p. 655–702.

8   Hamdani, M.R., S. Valcea, and M.R. Buckley, *The relentless pursuit of construct validity in the design of employment interviews*. Human Resource Management Review, 2014. **24**(2): p. 160–176.

9   Conway, J.M., R.A. Jako, and D.F. Goodman, *Meta-analysis of interrater and internal consistency reliability of selection interviews*. Journal of Applied Psychology, 1995. **80**(5): p. 565–579.

Setting the stage

The characteristics of high-quality interviews and how to prepare them

This is what a poorly designed job interview looks like ...

David is the director of the Research and Development department at Future Technology. His department recently received a budget increase from the company headquarters, and the decision was made to hire a new junior mechanical engineer with that money. After posting job advertisements in newspapers and online, David received a number of applications. He reviewed all resumes and selected four candidates for interviews. Sitting at his desk this morning, he looks at his agenda for the day and realizes that he has to interview Rachel at 9:30 a.m., Kareem at 11:00 a.m., and the other two candidates in the afternoon. David's background is in civil engineering. He has no formal training in interviewing (nor any other aspect of human resources), but he has interviewed a dozen job applicants since he was promoted to department director at Future Technology. His approach is quite straightforward. He starts the interview with a few questions from a list of the "ten best interview questions." He discovered them in a book about interviewing bought in an airport a few years ago. Then, he asks

DOI: 10.4324/9781003171089-2

additional questions based on the content of the applicant's resume and usually probes to get additional information when he is interested in the story told by the applicant.

Here are excerpts from David's interviews with both Rachel and Kareem:

Box 2.1

It is 9:30, and David welcomes Rachel in his office. After a few pleasantries, he starts with one of his usual questions: "So Rachel, what would you say are your strengths?"

Rachel immediately jumps in: "I am definitely a great team player. In engineering school, we often had to work on group projects, and I was always very comfortable collaborating with others. I also always tried to take the lead when possible – for instance, by assigning tasks to my teammates or sending email remainders about our deadlines. And I've also been playing on a volleyball team for about five years now, so teamwork is definitely part what I like to do!"

David is already impressed and continues with his second question: "OK, and what is your main weakness?"

Rachel is not surprised by this question and easily responds: "Well, I think that sometimes I can be too much of a perfectionist. I mean, I always work very hard to finalize everything perfectly, and I can be perceived as being over-conscientious to avoid any kind of mistake."

Satisfied with the information he has obtained, David picks up Rachel's resume and starts reviewing it: "Oh, I see that you worked as a summer intern for West Logistics last year. I know their operations director, Margaret Smith, quite well! We studied together. How was it to work there?"

Rachel replies directly: "Oh yes, Maggie! A very nice person and a great mentor; I liked working with her very much. It was

continued . . .

cont.

a great experience overall. Thanks to her, I've learned a lot about process optimization, managing supplies, etc."

David is delighted to hear that. "Yes, she is an excellent mentor for young engineers. I'm sure that you learned many things that could be very valuable here too."

The interview continues for another 40 minutes with David asking a few more questions about Rachel's experience at West Logistics, her training in general, and what made her apply to Future Technology in the first place. He concludes with a broader discussion about what working at the company would entail.

Box 2.2

A few minutes later, it is Kareem's time to interview. After a similar welcoming phase, David asks his first question: "So Kareem, what would you say is your main weakness?"

Kareem does not expect such a question at the start of the interview and hesitates before answering: "Oh, my main weakness ... It's a tough one! I could say that in the past I occasionally had difficulties dealing with conflictual situations. For instance, when someone would disagree with my idea, I would often back off instead of fighting for my idea. But this is something I've worked on recently, and I think that I was able to overcome this issue. Now I'm much better at this."

David is not entirely convinced but moves to a second question: "All right ... and where do you see yourself five years from now?"

Kareem thinks about it for a few seconds and then replies: "I hope to be working for Future Technology and maybe be in charge of an important project for the company. I mean, if I

continued . . .

cont.

prove myself during the first few years, I imagine that I will be given more responsibilities – maybe a promotion down the line or managing my own team of engineers for an important project."

David sees ambition but also some impatience in this answer. He then looks at Kareem's resume: "I can see that you participated in a robot competition when you were at your university. I never really understood those things. What got you involved in this?"

Kareem is actually very proud of this experience and tries to explain it: "I have always been interested in technology, I mean since I was a kid. And this competition was a chance to work with other engineers to build a robot from scratch and go to a national competition and show that our robot was better than the ones built by teams from other schools. It was a nice way to apply some of the theories I learnt in class, to implement some concepts in practice. I really enjoyed it."

Although David understands the practical interest of this activity, he is not completely sold. The interview continues for another 30 minutes or so. Kareem is asked some more questions about his experiences and choices, and David provides general information about working at Future Technology.

... and this is why it is ineffective

The two examples of job interviews may look familiar to you. You may have experienced similar interviews, either as an interviewer or as an applicant. So what is the problem here? There are actually a number of issues illustrated in those interviews. First, the interviewer (David) does not ask both candidates (Rachel and Kareem) the same questions. For instance, Rachel is asked about her strengths and weaknesses, whereas Kareem is questioned about his weakness and his vision for his future. As such, David obtained different pieces of information that cannot be directly compared. He knows Rachel's strengths but not Kareem's, and he knows Kareem's future vision but not Rachel's. It is possible that Rachel's plan for the future is better (or worse) than Kareem's, but David is left guessing about it. Similarly, the resume-based questions allow David to collect information about the candidates' past experiences, but he asks questions about very different situations. Once again, it is unclear how (or if) this information can be compared. Moreover, asking questions in a different order may influence applicants' answers, especially if some questions are more difficult than others. For instance, the *weakness* question could be distressing for some candidates, and answering it first may prevent them from making a good initial impression. The interview was easier for Rachel than for Kareem because she was asked about *strengths* first. Altogether, it would be difficult for David to effectively assess whether Rachel or Kareem is the best candidate for the job based on the information he obtained.

Second, the questions David asked were not clearly associated with job requirements. Ideally, an interviewer must collect information about candidates' qualifications that are necessary to perform the job or about their adequacy with the organization's values. This is what I described as P-J or P-O fit in Chapter 1. Mechanical engineers at Future Technology may need to possess specific knowledge, skills, and abilities, such as advanced knowledge of mathematical formulas or machines design, critical thinking skills, or the ability to combine pieces of information to reach optimal conclusions. They may also need to associate with the core values of the organization, such as having a thirst for innovation. However, the questions presented in the two examples above do not provide David with information that would allow him to evaluate if applicants possess those characteristics, making it difficult assess the degree of P-J or P-O fit. For instance, it is unclear if the strengths or weaknesses described by the applicants are related to the junior engineer position. It is possible that some candidates will mention strengths or weaknesses that are job-related, but the process of obtaining this information is not followed consistently. For instance, teamwork is perhaps important at Future Technology, yet only Rachel (but not Kareem) had the opportunity to mention it. If teamwork is a key aspect of the job, then David should directly ask a question assessing candidates' experience working in teams.

Third, some of the questions are so popular that applicants can provide rehearsed answers, which can prove meaningless for interviewers. Let's be honest. If interviewers rely on a list of the *best* questions they found online or in a book bought in an airport, it is likely that job applicants can access a similar list. Moreover, smart (or well-prepared) applicants have probably found websites or books describing the best strategies for answering those questions or even examples or responses to use in the interview.[1] For example, the vast majority *how-to* books about interviews will describe the *weakness* question and advise candidates to discuss either something that is actually a strength rather than a weakness (e.g., Rachel being a perfectionist) or a past weakness that the candidate has overcome (e.g., Kareem's improved persuasion skills). In both cases, David did not obtain valid information about the job-related qualities of candidates.

Fourth and finally, David's approach creates opportunities for some candidates to positively influence his evaluation and also highlights potential biases towards others. By asking Rachel about her recent experience working with someone he knows personally, he offers her an easy chance to shine. Rachel jumps on that opportunity to impress him. Knowing that David and her former supervisor are close (i.e., he openly stated that they studied together) helped Rachel to create an impression of closeness with David. For instance, by calling her former supervisor "Maggie," she stressed how close their relationship was (or still is). Moreover, she highlights that Maggie was a great mentor and that she learnt a lot from her. Rachel thus has the chance to engage in an influence tactic called *ingratiation*, which can positively impact David's assessment.[2] However, David never offered such an opportunity to Kareem. Instead, he chooses to ask Kareem to describe an experience (i.e., the robot competition) for which he blatantly admits a lack of interest (i.e., "I never really understood those things"). As such, he forces Kareem to defend or justify his involvement in such an activity in order to protect his image as a qualified candidate. Such defensive tactics, although necessary for the candidate, are likely to negatively impact David's assessment.[3]

If David's approach to interviewing candidates is suboptimal, what should he do to make it better? The solution involves introducing more structure in the interview process. Decades of employment interview research have highlighted the value of *structured interviews* (over an *unstructured* format, like David's approach).[4] While there is some evidence that some unstructured interviews can be somewhat valid, structured interviews are generally much more valid (i.e., up to two times higher predictive validity), more reliable (i.e., 20–30% increase in agreements between interviewers), and less prone to biases.[5] In the next sections, I describe different techniques that interviewers can use to structure the interview process. I also explain why those technique help make interviews more effective, describe their psychological foundations, and highlight the numerous advantages (but also the potential drawbacks) associated with each technique. I also emphasize how applicants can prepare for structured interviews.

Increasing interview objectivity and fairness through standardization

One core aspect of structured interviews involves developing a standardized process, which should be used in a similar fashion when interviewing all applicants for a specific position. For instance, the same process should be followed when interviewing Rachel, Kareem, and the other two candidates for the junior engineer position at Future Technology. As a first step, the same interviewer must prepare all questions in advance of the interview and ask all applicants for the same job the same questions in the same order. Such an approach forces interviewers to develop questions designed to assess job-specific knowledge, skills, and abilities or the stable traits and values important to the organization (more on this in the next sections). At the same time, it prevents interviewers from asking question "on the fly" or based on the unique experiences of an applicant (i.e., based on the content of their resume).

This approach could be frustrating for interviewers who are used to having more freedom during the interview or who like to learn more about each applicant individually.[6] Yet, this approach has a number of advantages. First, by asking Rachel, Kareem, and the other candidates the same questions, the interviewer can collect comparable information from all of them. If questions are accurately capturing job requirements (in other words, they have high construct validity), each piece of information should be valuable when evaluating which applicant is the best suited for the position. Interviewers can thus analyse, compare, or score the collected information in a systematic way to make an informed decision. As a result, this approach increases the likelihood of hiring the applicant who possesses all the qualities necessary to become a productive member of the organization. For instance, David could evaluate the critical thinking or analytical skills of all four candidates by asking them the same question(s) and comparing how the applicants performed on the question(s) to determine who is likely more qualified for the mechanical engineer position.

Second, a standardized approach reduces the risk of biases and errors associated with the interview. Interviewers are human beings, and their appreciation of job applicants is, by definition, subjective. In some situations, they may try to favour a particular candidate who possesses specific characteristics that they like (e.g., Rachel worked with someone David knows and appreciates). Or they may try to question the activities or preferences of another candidate (e.g., Kareem's passion for robot competitions). Using a standardized interview protocol with prepared questions prevents such instances from occurring. Unlike in the interview examples presented above, it will not be possible to direct easier (or more complex) questions to applicants that the interviewer likes (or dislikes) or create opportunities for only some applicants to make a good impression.

A final, but related, advantage of a standardized approach is it increases the fairness of the interviewing process. Because all applicants are asked the same questions (and should be evaluated the same way – but see the section below about using rating scales), organizations are better protected against cases of unfair treatment, discrimination, nepotism, and the like. Indeed, candidates not hired by David could argue that they were not evaluated fairly because they were asked more difficult questions than other candidates. Such a situation can particularly hurt the organization when overlooked applicants are members of protected groups (e.g., women, seniors, ethnic or racial minorities, disabled, etc.). Members of those groups (and others) are legally protected against discrimination in many countries or regions, including the European Union (Charter of Fundamental Rights), the U.K. (Equality Act), the U.S. (Civil Rights Act), and Canada (Human Rights Act). The organization could be sued by disregarded applicants who perceive discrimination. A standardized approach acts as a shield protecting the organization because it ensures the consistent treatment of all candidates. There is plenty of evidence from legal cases showing that the court is more likely to rule in favour of the hiring organization when it relied on a standardized approach to assess all candidates.[7]

Using panel interviews because two heads are better than one

A second key characteristic of high-quality interviews is to rely on a panel.[8] Panel interviews are conducted by two or more interviewers. Such a format has a number of advantages compared to one-on-one interviews. First, conducting an interview is a cognitively complex task when done alone because the interviewer has to ask a question, listen to the response, assess its quality and the information obtained, and prepare the next question. Adding additional tasks, such as taking notes, can be a burden when the interviewer is alone. Indeed, the interviewer likely wants to engage in active listening to show interest in the applicant's response, which requires making eye contact or nodding. Such non-verbal behaviours are often incompatible with effective note taking. In panel interviews, information gathering can be improved by assigning roles to each interviewer. For instance, while one interviewer asks a question and attentively listens to the applicant's response, another interviewer can take detailed descriptive notes based on the response. The roles can be set for the entire interview, or interviewers can switch roles for each question (i.e., A asks the first question while B takes notes, then B asks the second question while A takes notes). Both interviewers can then discuss and assess the responses using those notes at the end of the interview. Having multiple interviewers thus reduces the risk that job-relevant information is missed or voluntarily ignored, while at the same time it ensures that at least one interviewer is actively listening to the applicant. This leads to two positive outcomes for the organization: better information-gathering, which increases the likelihood of making more valid decisions, and potentially better reactions from applicants.

Relatedly, panel interviews are also more resistant to biases and errors, mostly because interviewers can check on each other to ensure that irrelevant information does not influence the decision.[9] For instance, as mentioned earlier, interview outcomes can sometimes be impacted by interviewers' biases against certain groups (e.g., seniors or ethnic minorities). Such biases are rarely explicit, and even the most prejudiced interviewers can hide their negative reactions. However, even implicit biases can still indirectly influence hiring decisions and lead to cases of discrimination. Panel interviews may thus provide organizations with a second layer of legal protection and reduce the risk of discrimination because decisions are reviewed by other interviewers. Indeed, using panel interviews has been related to positive court outcomes for organizations. Also, working with multiple interviewers allows for members of protected groups to be represented. Organizations are encouraged to include interviewers of different genders, ages, or races/ethnicities in the panel. For instance, a panel of three interviewers composed of a 50-year-old White man, a 35-year-old Black woman, and a 25-year-old Asian man would ensure a process that incorporates multiple perspectives and advertises the organization's diversity. It can also enhance applicants' perceptions of fairness and their interest in the job.

Making the interview job-related with behavioural questions

Using a standardized approach and a panel of interviewers creates an optimal environment to support an effective interview, but the interview's value will ultimately depend on the quality of the questions asked. It is like forming a rock band. A *good* band needs talented musicians playing with high-quality instruments, but a *great* band needs a brilliant singer at the centre of the stage! In this section, I will describe how organizations can develop *great* interview questions using the behavioural approach.[10]

As a starting point, it seems important to clarify what the concept of behavioural interviewing does *not* involve. This approach is *not* about observing or analysing the behaviours of the applicant during the interview. Interviewers are *not* asked to play Sherlock Holmes and investigate or interpret body movements or signs of anxiety from applicants to assess them. Instead, behavioural interviewing means that applicants will be invited to talk about the way they behave at work. Behavioural questions are also very different from traditional or popular interview questions. Like David's *ten best* questions (e.g., "What is your greatest strength?"), traditional questions are often oriented towards applicants' generic descriptions of their qualities, their preferred work styles, or their career ambitions. As mentioned above, such questions are often not job related. And, even when they are associated with job requirements, they only ask candidates to describe *what* they do well (or, rather, what they *think* they do well) and not *how* they do it. In other words, such traditional questions encourage applicants to tell interviewers what skills or abilities they think they possess, but the questions do not ask directly for demonstrations of how candidates have used these skills in the past (or would use them on the job). Sometimes applicants' statements are valid indicators of their actual qualities, but at times they can also be exaggerations or even blatant inventions. Anyone can say that they are excellent leaders or communicators!

This is when behavioural interviewing takes the stage! Such a technique is built on the idea that the best way to gather information about applicants in an interview involves asking them how they applied (or would apply) specific skills to solve particular job-related problems. This approach is not new – industrial psychologists developed the idea of behavioural interviewing more than 40 years ago – and psychological research has accumulated evidence about its validity and reliability.[11] Indeed, as compared to the traditional questions described above, a behavioural approach allows interviewers to gather more information. It is also likely to help collect more valid information because it is much more difficult for applicants to mislead interviewers when they have to answer a question asking them to describe precisely what they did or would do, as compared to questions asking them what skills they possess.

In order to create valid behavioural questions, interviewers have to go through an initial information-gathering stage to learn more about the job. Organizations can use various approaches, including processes called *job analyses* or *competency modeling*.[12] Overall, the main goal is to understand the key features of the job and the type of knowledge, skills, abilities, competencies, or other individual characteristics that are necessary to perform the job. When organizations want to use behavioural interviews, a pertinent approach to achieve this objective is to rely on the *critical incident technique*. This technique involves identifying a series of job-related situations that are *critical* – that is, situations that can be handled very effectively by competent employees but ineffectively by less competent ones. All jobs involve a large number of *non-critical* situations that most employees (even the less competent ones) can handle easily. *Critical* incidents can be less frequent, but their impact on the employees' performance (and indirectly their team or the whole organization) is much more significant.

Interviewers may thus need to identify a few job-specific *critical* situations and understand what behaviours would represent adequate (vs. inadequate) responses to those situations. Interviewers can interrogate experts on the job, such as the current job incumbents or their supervisors, who are generally privy to such situations and adequate responses. The appropriate behaviours are usually associated with job-related skills or competencies that can be assessed using behavioural interview questions. By talking to number of employees, some very qualified high-performers and other less effective individuals, managers can also identify the effective and ineffective reactions. The box below presents some examples of how a hiring manager can collect critical incidents from employees.

Box 2.3 HOW TO GATHER CRITICAL INCIDENTS FROM EMPLOYEES

What would you describe as the most complex, difficult, or stressful situation you encouter in your job? It does not need to be a regular occurrence, but when it happens it is the kind of situation that has a massive impact on you, your colleagues, our customers, or the company in general. Please describe the

continued . . .

---

cont.

situation in detail and explain why it is so impactful. Then, tell me how you generally respond to such a situation and why.

Please think about an experience in your current role that represents one of your best accomplishments. When you have identified that situation, give me a broad overview of how you got involved in it, who the other players were, and what the nature of the task was. Then, tell me what you did. Please walk me through your actions step by step and go into as much detail as possible.

Take the example of a flight attendant job. Most flight attendants are perfectly capable of greeting passengers, checking their boarding passes and passports, and serving meals and drinks. Those are *non-critical* situations that all attendants usually perform adequately. However, *critical* situations may involve communicating with passengers when the plane is facing heavy turbulence or when the flight is delayed, dealing with a drunk or aggressive passenger, or helping a passenger who is sick. These situations are less frequent (they may not occur in all flights), but dealing with them adequately requires specific job-related skills or competencies. For instance, in all those situations, flight attendants should remain calm, manage their emotions, and communicate effectively. Ideally, interview questions for flight-attendant positions should help assess those particular skills – for instance, by asking candidates to describe how they have dealt (or would deal) with similar *critical* situations.

The same approach could be used by David to develop interview questions for the mechanical engineer job at Future Technology. David may already possess a good idea of the critical situations for the job, being an engineer himself and being in charge of the department. But he could also collect critical incidents from mechanical engineers currently working in the department or their direct supervisors. For instance, a *critical* situation for that job could involve a project with a deadline that has been shortened or a budget that has been reduced at the last minute, but for which clients still expect high-quality deliverables. Engineers must possess excellent organizational and time-management skills to be able to handle such a situation effectively. David can thus create a question asking Rachel, Kareem, and the other two applicants how they have managed (or would manage) a situation in which their resources (e.g., money, time, manpower) were unexpectedly reduced.

Behavioural interviews are built upon critical incidents (and associated adequate responses) in order to discover how job applicants behave in such situations. To obtain an approximation of such behaviours, some organizations rely on instruments like Assessment Centres or work sample tests in an attempt to replicate critical situations in a simulated environment. For instance, in Assessment Centre exercises an applicant for a managerial position could be asked to solve problems, deliver a presentation in front of evaluators, or deal with difficult employees in a role play. Alternatively, an applicant for a secretary position can be asked to type a text as fast and as accurately as possible. However, such instruments are often too costly for organizations (e.g., an Assessment Center can be very complex and expensive to organize), they may be irrelevant for the specific job (e.g., it is difficult to design work-sample tests for managerial roles), or the critical incidents are impossible to practically replicate (e.g., recreating the stress and risks associated with entering a building on fire for firefighters). In such cases, behavioural interviews are the next best thing. Below I describe two alternative forms of behavioural interviews: past-behavioural interviews (also known as patterned behaviour description interviews) and situational interviews.

Using past-behavioural interview questions

This approach relies on a general principle established through decades of psychological research: *The best predictor of future behaviour is past behaviour.* This implies that if someone was able to use specific knowledge, skills, or abilities to achieve something in the past, they should be able to replicate the same behaviour again in the future when facing a similar situation. For instance, someone who was able to solve a problem, help another person, or communicate something effectively in their last job is likely to possess the qualities required to reiterate the same behaviour in their next job. The ideal approach to assess if applicants possess those desirable qualities would be to directly observe them demonstrating those qualities through actions (or behaviours) – that is, observe what they have done. Unfortunately, we do not have magical time-traveling abilities, and I have not yet seen an operational version of Doc Brown's DeLorean form *Back to the Future*. Therefore, we cannot go back in time and observe what candidates did in the past.

Using a job interview as our main instrument, the best solution available involves asking the applicant to report such past behaviours. Interviewers are thus encouraged to design past-behavioural questions. Such questions ask applicants to describe precisely how they behaved in specific *critical* situations (ideally at work, but also in other contexts) in the past, focusing on experiences where they successfully applied job-related qualities. For instance, past-behavioural questions often start with "Tell me about a time when you…." Because past behaviours predict future behaviours, interviewers can assess the appropriateness of the described past behaviours for the job the candidates applied for. If those behaviours correspond to what the organization expects from a competent employee in similar *critical* situations (i.e., if the applicant demonstrated possessing and using the appropriate skills or competencies), the applicant's response will be positively evaluated.

If we go back to the task of interviewing candidates for the mechanical engineer position at Future Technology, David could design a number of past-behavioural questions to assess whether Rachel, Kareem, and the other two applicants possess the necessary qualities for the position. For instance, I described earlier the *critical* situation of managing a project with a shortened deadline or budget. The ideal candidate must thus demonstrate *time management* or *organization* skills. Therefore, David could say to candidates, "Tell me about a time when you had to manage multiple tasks or projects with competing deadlines and limited time and/or resources available. What was the situation? How did you handle it?"

Below, I present a few examples of past-behavioural questions to assess competencies that can be valuable for a variety of jobs. I include more examples in the "Toolbox" at the end of the chapter. Although interviewers may be tempted to use the questions directly, it is still recommended that they follow the process described above to identify *critical* situations and key skills or competencies specific to the job they are hiring for before deciding if (some of) the example questions are appropriate for them or if they have to develop new questions.

Box 2.4

- *Problem-solving*: Describe a project for which you faced an unexpected roadblock. What was the problem, and how did you deal with it to move forward?
- *Communication*: Tell me about a time when you had to communicate something to someone whose knowledge of English was limited. How did you manage to get your message across?
- *Teamwork*: Tell me about a team-based project where some tensions, disagreements, or conflicts started to emerge. How did the group handle the situation, and what was you role in that process?
- *Leadership*: Describe a time when you were either put in charge or decided to take charge of a group of people to achieve a common goal. What happened?

In the examples above, I often include one or two specific element(s) that the applicant is instructed to describe in their answer – for instance, what the situation was or what they did. How much guidance to provide candidates is an issue that is often debated by job-interview researchers. In other words, whether or not an interviewer should follow-up initial past-behavioural questions with probes to help applicants complete their answer.[13] On the one hand, proponents of highly standardized forms of interviews have argued that probing creates opportunities for interviewers' biases to influence evaluations. For instance, some applicants could be asked follow-up questions that can help them improve their initial answer, whereas others may not be offered this opportunity. Interviewers can sometimes even use probing as a way to push back on applicants' original responses – for example, by questioning the veracity of the experience shared by the applicants. As a result, some of the biases the organization has tried to eliminate with a standardized interview protocol could come back into the game and influence the interview process and hiring decisions.

On the other hand, some researchers (and many hiring professionals) have argued that probing may be an effective way to gather more job-related information about the candidate, thus helping interviewers make more valid hiring decisions. If chosen appropriately, follow-up questions can be instrumental in obtaining more precise information about the situation faced by the applicant, their behaviour, or the outcome that resulted. The more data that is gathered, the more likely interviewers can make an informed decision about the applicants' suitability for the job. Moreover, by increasing applicants' accountability, probing can also be used to reduce opportunities for deception to occur.

If interviewers want to use probing, the best approach is to use it in a systematic way. For instance, the situation-task-action-result (or STAR) method can be used to help gather more consistent (and thus comparable) information from all applicants. Applicants can be asked follow-up questions to clarify the situation or problem they faced (the "S"); their role, position, responsibilities, or the task they were expected to accomplish (the "T"); the actions they took or the decision they made (the "A"); and the result or outcome they obtained (the "R"). Interviewers can thus use probes when applicants did not provide enough information about one (or several) of the four aspects. For instance, if the applicant did not provide enough details about the "T" and "R" parts when answering the leadership question described above, the interviewer could ask: "You mentioned that you were successful in leading your team. How many members were in that team? And what outcomes did your team achieve?"

An alternative to using probing questions is to provide instructions to all applicants at the beginning of (or before) the interview. For instance, applicants can be told that they will be asked to describe past experiences, and interviewers will expect them to structure their answers around the following four points: (1) the situation they encountered, (2) their role or the task they had to perform, (3) the actions they took, and (4) the results they obtained. Such instructions ensure that all applicants structure their answers in a similar way and provide complete information (or at least it provides all applicants with the opportunity to do so). It can also help applicants to perform at their best during the interview. For example, research has shown that applicants who structure their responses using the STAR approach are evaluated more positively during interviews.[14] Those who were coached to follow the STAR structure before interviewing perform better during the interview.[15] As such, from a candidate's perspective, it would also be beneficial to use this technique even when not instructed to do so by the interviewer.

Past-behavioural interviews have a number of qualities. As mentioned above, they allow interviewers to collect extensive information about applicants' past behaviours (usually in work situations) and, indirectly, the skills or competencies they possess. Moreover, research has highlighted that such interviews are highly reliable and can be quite valid (i.e., help accurately predict job performance).[16] However, past-behavoural interviews also have some weaknesses. Most importantly, there are situations for which using the psychological principle at the core of this approach (i.e., that past behaviours predict future behaviours) is simply impossible to apply. For instance, when interviewing for low-skill or entry-level positions that do not require prior experience, many applicants may not have past experiences they can rely on to respond. For instance, young graduates from business schools applying for junior management positions may never have held jobs where they had to manage a team or projects before. In such situations, applicants are encouraged to rely on non-work experiences, such as student groups, clubs, sports teams, or volunteering activities, but such situations can be less relevant for the position.

Similarly, some jobs may also be so unique (or involve dealing with situations that are specific to the job, organization, or industry) that even seasoned candidates would not have experienced something similar in their past positions. For instance, an engineer applying for a position at a space agency (e.g., NASA, ESA, or even private organizations like Space-X or Virgin Galactic) likely would have never worked on rockets or space shuttles before. Therefore, their past experience may not be directly pertinent for the position they apply for. Moreover, it is likely that the experiences described by the applicants will be so heterogenous that attempting to compare applicants will become virtually impossible. Fortunately, psychology research has developed an alternative form of behavioural interview that does not suffer from the limitations highlighted above: situational interviews.

Using situational interview questions

Situational interviews are based on a second principle derived from psy-chology research: *People tend to do what they say*. This principle is based on goal-setting theory, which argues that intentions (i.e., what people say) are related to behaviour (i.e., what people do) because setting specific goals tends to motivate people to perform better in order to achieve them.[17] If one can precisely measure job-related intentions, such intentions can serve as valid indicators or predictors of on-the-job behaviours. Interestingly, research in neuroscience has also garnered evidence that what goes on at the neurological level (e.g., what areas of the brain are activated) is very similar to what goes on when one is imagining complex actions or actually engaging in those same actions.[18] Applied to the interview context, the *people tend to do what they say* principle suggests that the alternative to asking applicants to describe how they behaved in the past is to design questions allowing them to describe precisely how they would behave in a hypothetical situation that could happen on the job (in the future). The reasoning behind the situational interview technique is that applicants who are able to describe the right way to deal with a particular issue should also be able (and motivated) to behave accordingly when such an issue actually arises at work.

Hypothetical situations presented to applicants can be written in a way that closely depicts the critical incidents collected from the job experts. This has a number of positive effects. First, by increasing the realism associated with the questions, situational interviews can achieve very high levels of construct validity (i.e., they are strongly job related). Second, all applicants are tackling exactly the same issue in the same (hypothetical) situation, which facilitates direct comparisons between applicants' responses and ensures that all responses will be job relevant. With past-behavioural questions, it is more likely that applicants will describe very different experiences that can be more difficult to compare and less relevant for the job. Finally, probing or follow-up questions are usually superfluous because the situation and task are provided to the applicants, who are only asked to describe their intended actions.

One important caveat associated with situational questions is that interviewers' assessments are based on proposed behaviours only. With past-behavioural questions, applicants have to rely on existing experience and accomplishments, or they have to describe actual problems they solved in the past. In other words, there is some evidence that they can behave a certain way. With situational questions, however, they are only asked to solve hypothetical problems. As such, some people can say that they would do something, but never *walk the talk* once on the job. For instance, a candidate could say that they would stay late to finish an important project on time (if they believe that this is what the interviewer expects), knowing that they would never actually do so. Therefore, a key feature of effective situational interviews is to include complexity or some form of dilemma to reduce the transparency of the question, so that candidates cannot simply provide a good answer without consequences. The purpose of the dilemma is to make individuals more likely to describe what they believe they would actually do in a given work situation and thus minimize the risk that they provide a socially desirable response.[19] Therefore, effective situational questions should not have an *easy* or *desirable* solution. Applicants must be able to demonstrate that they possess the required knowledge to act appropriately, describe precisely how they would act, and highlight the steps they would take to ensure that a positive outcome is achieved.

Let's use again the example of David's interview with mechanical engineer candidates. He can use a situational question to assess their ability to manage a project with a shortened deadline or budget (i.e., their *time management* or *organization* skills). David could thus ask candidates the following question.

Box 2.5

"Imagine that you are in charge of the following project: You have to design a new high-efficiency industrial electric generator for a client. You have been working on this project for two months now, and you have one month left to present your final report. You have the next steps clearly laid out, and you believe that you are on track to finish it just in time if you work full-time on it. However, your supervisor informs you that the client is facing financial difficulties and has reduced the budget invested in the project. As such, your boss suggests that you allocate only half of your time next month to finishing your report and gives you another project to start working on. How would you proceed?"

Below, I present a few other examples of situational questions, each designed to assess a particular competency for a specific job and organization (or industry). More examples are included in the "Toolbox" at the end of the chapter. These examples should give the reader a good idea of what such questions can look like. However (and even more so than with examples of past-behavioural questions), it is recommended that interviewers identify *critical* situations and key skills or competencies unique to the specific job rather than directly using the examples listed below.

Box 2.6

- *Leadership (for a supervisor in construction)*: You are in charge of a team of ten professionals working on constructing a new building. An electrician and a carpenter start arguing over an installation issue, each blaming the other for the problem. The carpenter storms out of the room while yelling insults, and the electrician comes to you claiming that working with the carpenter is now impossible. How would you approach this situation?

- *Teamwork (for a sales associate)*: You are working as a sales associate at a electronics store. After working for several weeks in the television department, your boss put you in charge of the mobile phone department. You are very busy with a large delivery of new phones that needs to be checked, updated in the inventory management system, and displayed on the shelves. While walking to the back of the store to check the phone delivery, you notice Pat, a new employee in the television department, who looks confused and seems to be struggling with an increasingly agitated customer. What would you do?

- *Decision-making (for a flight attendant)*: You are the senior flight attendant (or purser) on a direct 13-hour flight between London and Singapore. You and your team just finished serving a mid-flight meal. As you plan to start serving extra drinks, you see one of your junior colleagues

---

continued . . .

cont.

running towards you in a state of panic. They explain that a passenger is apparently having a severe allergic reaction to something they ate. When you approach the passenger, they seem agitated and out of breath. Before the passenger can explain anything to you, they suddenly lose consciousness. What would your course of action be?

- *Resilience/Problem-solving (for a marketing expert)*: You arrive at the office at 8:00 a.m. At 9:00 a.m., your team is scheduled to present a pitch for a new marketing campaign to a very important client in the meeting room. For the last month, you have been working on this proposal alongside three colleagues: Amir, Brandy, and Chris. While the project was initially progressing well, one week ago Chris unexpectedly got sick and had to abandon the project. As such, Amir, Brandy, and you had to work extra hours to ensure the project's completion. You stayed in the office until 11:00 p.m. last night to finalize it. Each of you is in charge of presenting a third of the pitch. While rehearsing your part of the pitch, you get a text from Brandy at 8:30 a.m. She was involved in a car accident on her way to work and has to go to the hospital to check for a concussion. The meeting is in 30 minutes. How would you handle this situation?

- *Communication (for a financial advisor)*: You are meeting for the first time with a customer to discuss potential investment opportunities. When reviewing the customer's chequing account, you realize that while the individual has a substantial sum of money in the account, they have no other types of accounts or investments. You believe that there is potential to invest some of the customer's money more effectively, for instance on the stock market. However, when you start describing several investment options, the customer looks completely puzzled. After asking some questions, you realize that the customer's English skills are limited. How would you approach this situation?

Both situational and past-behavioural questions have a number of strengths, but also a few weaknesses. Existing research suggests that both demonstrate high (and similar) levels of reliability and acceptable-to-high (and also similar) levels of predictive validity.[20] For instance, interviews relying on situational or past-behavioural questions usually score between 25 and 40 (out of 100) on the prediction scale described in Chapter 1, but this level can increase when behavioural questions are associated with the other features of high-quality interviews described earlier (and in the next section). The main difference is that each question type seems to be capturing different constructs (or qualities). Situational questions capture job knowledge and (to some extent) cognitive abilities, whereas past-behavioural questions capture job experience and (to some extent) personality traits. Moreover, as described earlier, past-behavioural questions require applicants to describe evidence of actual behaviours in the past, but such experiences may sometimes be of limited pertinence for the future job. Situational questions, however, contain situations that are extremely job relevant, but they lack the demonstration part. Therefore, it can be valuable to design a comprehensive interview integrating both types of questions.

Effectively evaluating applicants' responses with rating scales

The last touch to create a high-quality interview involves developing an effective measure to assess applicants' responses. Using a standardized approach and a panel of interviewers reduces many biases, and using behavioural questions ensures that more relevant information is collected from applicants. However, optimal hiring decisions can only be achieved if the information gathered in the interview is assessed and used appropriately by the interviewer(s). Unfortunately, organizations sometimes overlook this aspect of the interview design and leave interviewers with the difficult task of integrating all the information provided by applicants in their responses to reach a decision. This can lead to many problems. For instance, pertinent information can be forgotten or ignored, some pieces of information can be weighted more heavily than others without a valuable justification, decisions can be based on overall evaluations instead of specific facts about the candidate, or interviewers' personal preferences or biases can influence decisions. To avoid such undesirable issues, interviewers can use *anchored rating scales* to help them score applicants' responses, compare applicants, and reach a more objective hiring decision.

Anchored rating scales can be developed together with each behavioural question. Although the content of the scale will be slightly different for past-behavioural vs. situational questions, the format and use of rating scales will be the same. Their goal is to allow interviewers to translate their assessment of applicants' responses to each question into a score. It is important to note that interviewers are not asked to score the applicant as an individual (or to reduce a person to a simple number), but to evaluate the quality or appropriateness of applicants' responses on a scale including a number of levels. As such, candidates' responses to the same question can be directly and easily compared. For instance, David could score Rachel's and Kareem's responses to the question about their organization skills and then compare their scores. Below I present examples of scales using five levels. Scales with more or fewer levels are also possible. However, using fewer than four levels could render the scale too imprecise to be effective, and using more than seven levels could make it too cumbersome.

Each level should be associated with increasingly appropriate responses – that is, more pertinent descriptions of past experiences and behaviours (for past-behavioural questions) or more adequate proposed behaviours for the given hypothetical situation (for situational questions). Ideally, the scale should incorporate a general definition and a specific illustration of responses/behaviours associated with each level of appropriateness. In other words, the scale should include a broad description of what a "Level 1" behaviour entails and a concrete example of an applicant's answer that would correspond to that level. The description and example should depict a behaviour that is particularly inappropriate. Alternatively, definitions and illustrations for Level 5 should represent ideal behaviours (and outcomes in the case of past-behavioural questions). Interviewers can thus use the scales to evaluate candidates' answers during the interview, or they can take detailed descriptive notes and score answers with the scale at the end of the interview. More precisely, they can use the descriptions and examples of behaviours for each level of the scale as benchmarks against which the applicants' responses can be compared. If the response resembles descriptions for Level 4, the candidate will get a score of 4.

Where do the behaviours and examples for all levels come from? They should be adapted from the information obtained from job experts during the collection of critical incidents. During that phase, job incumbents or supervisors provide the interviewer with descriptions of critical situations and examples of appropriate behaviours (and perhaps also inappropriate ones). For instance, David should have collected opinions and personal experiences about the best ways to deal with the shortened deadline situation during his discussions with mechanical engineers or their supervisors in the Research & Development department. Interviewers may have to fill potential gaps – for example, by creating content for the intermediate levels of the scale to ensure that the scale is complete. Sometime, creating definitions that are clearly different for all levels can be cumbersome. In that case, a scale with definitions for just Levels 1, 3, and 5 can be acceptable, if clearly different examples are provided for all levels.

I present below two examples of anchored rating scales (one past-behavioural and one situational question). Once again, those are only examples, and interviewers interested in using rating scales are encouraged to develop their own job-specific instruments.

From the applicants' perspective, there are also a few important lessons here. First, they should expect interviewers to rely on both past-behavioural and situational questions. Past-behavioural questions will be used to assess whether they possess job-relevant skills and abilities, thus applicants are expected to demonstrate skills and abilities through detailed descriptions of past work experiences and achievements. Situational questions will assess their capacity to adequately react to various workplace situations and issues, requiring applicants to carefully consider the context, actors at play, and the best approach to follow. Second, applicants should expect interviewers to take notes while they speak and/or assess their responses against a standardized scoring system. The more detailed their response is (particularly for past-behavioural questions), and the more they can describe their thought process or problem-solving approach (especially for situational questions), the more likely they will hit the key points in the scoring system. In summary, for applicants a successful interview requires a combination of relevant experience, understanding the questions, and communicating responses effectively.

Table 2.1 – Example rating scale for past-behavioural question

Skill assessed	Communication	
Past-behavioural question: Tell me about a time when you had to explain something complex (for instance a complex concept or the technical features of an object) to someone who was not familiar with it.		
Score	**Behaviour description**	**Example response**
1	Presents a situation where the concept or feature explained was **not complex** at all and/or **did not necessitate adapting** one's communication style.	As an engineer, I explained an electrical component to another engineer. I explained the technical features, and my colleague understood the concept immediately.
2	Presents a situation where the concept or feature explained was **complex** and the target was not an expert, but the person **failed to properly adapt** their **communication style**.	As an engineer, I explained an electrical component to a client. I used technical terms or jargon when explaining the features to highlight my expertise.
3	Presents a situation where the concept or feature explained was **complex** and the target was not an expert. The person **tried to adapt** their **communication style**, but was only **partially successful** at making the message clear to the target.	As an engineer, I explained an electrical component to a client. I used lay terms to make technical features simpler, but the client was not fully convinced and/or was not clear about the value added by this component.
4	Presents a situation where the person had to explain **something really complex** to a novice, was able to **take** the novice's **perspective**, **adapted the communication style** and language used, but **did not make sure** that the novice **understood**.	As an engineer, I explained an electrical component to a client. I avoided jargon and used lay terms to make technical features simpler. I believe that the client did understand (and assume that it was clear).

continued . . .

(Continued)

Skill assessed	Communication	
5	Presents a situation where the person had to explain **something really complex** to a novice, was able to **take** the novice's **perspective, adapted the communication style** and language used, and then **made sure** that the novice **understood**.	As an engineer, I explained an electrical component to a client. I avoided jargon and used lay terms to make technical features simpler. After my explanation I asked the client a few questions to make sure they understood, and I made sure that everything was clear by asking them to repeat a few key points.

Table 2.2 – Example rating scale for situational question

Skill assessed	Managing pressure	
Situational question: You are the assistant manager of a bar at an international airport. The weather is very bad today, and you hear an announcement that all departing flights will be delayed for the next four to five hours. It is likely that an unusually high number of passengers will come to your bar to drink or eat something while waiting. How do you react in this situation?		
Score	**Behaviour description**	**Example response**
1	Expects to face a stressful situation **without making any specific change**.	Anticipates a large number of clients and realizes that the next few hours will be stressful. Yet, no further analysis of the situation is conducted, and no changes are made to adapt (e.g., about stocks, number of employees).
2	Anticipates an issue to arise, but only engages in **minimal actions** without collecting all necessary information.	Takes the newly received information into account and supposes that there may be not enough food supplies at the bar. Sends a waiter to obtain additional supplies in the stocks or in a store.

continued . . .

(Continued)

Skill assessed	Managing pressure	
3	Tries to quickly **obtain a proxy of the information** required to do one's job and **evaluates the overall needs** and changes to make.	Looks at the number of delayed flights to estimate the number of passengers and thus additional customers. Quickly estimates the required supplies and compares this number to supplies available at the bar. Calls people in charge of stocks or delivery to ask about the availability of additional supplies.
4	Obtains **pertinent information** to do one's job effectively, evaluates the overall needs, and **acts on required adaptations**.	Talks with flight attendants to obtain a general estimation of the number of delayed passengers. Compares this number to supplies available at the bar. If necessary, calls people in charge of stocks or delivery to obtain additional emergency supplies.
5	**Analyzes** the potential gap between requirements and available resources, **takes the initiative** to obtain useful and necessary information to **make appropriate decisions**, and engages in an appropriate process to solve the problem.	Contacts airport administration or airlines to obtain a precise number of delayed passengers and more information about the delay. Compares this number to supplies available at the bar. If necessary, calls people in charge of stocks or delivery to obtain additional emergency supplies. Calls additional (part-time) employees to come help with service.

Once interviewers have scored the responses to each question for all applicants, they can engage in a number of analyses to help them make a decision. First, they can compare all candidates on individual questions – for instance, to identify which one scored higher for a very important job qualification (e.g., which one of the four candidates for the mechanical engineer job scored higher for *organization* skills). They can also calculate an overall interview score for each candidate by adding the scores for all questions and comparing the overall scores of all candidates to identify the best one. Note that interviewers can decide (ideally beforehand) to give more weight to questions about the most important qualifications, although they should be able to justify such decisions. For instance, if David asked his candidates six behavioural questions, he could double the points for questions about *organization* and *critical thinking* when calculating overall scores.

The benefits associated with using anchored rating scales are numerous.[21] First, using such scales reduces interviewers' cognitive and memory demands, as they can use behaviours and examples from each level as benchmarks to assess applicants' responses. As such, their assessment of applicants is made easier, the decision is based on more precise information, and the interview is thus likely to be more valid. Second, scales reduce the impact of interviewers' biases (or preferences) by providing a standard to evaluate all applicants. This helps increase the reliability of the interview – for instance, because multiple interviewers in a panel are more likely to agree on evaluations than without scales. Finally, rating scales scores provide the organization with more objective data to justify hiring decision and protect themselves against lawsuits from rejected candidates.

The characteristics of high-quality interviews: Summary

In this chapter, I described the various issues associated with sub-optimal forms of interviews, highlighting how traditional questions could create opportunities for biases while potentially preventing interviewers from gathering job-related information to make effective hiring decisions. I then explained how interviewers can design high-quality interviews based on decades of research conducted by industrial psychology or management scholars. In order to summarize the key features of such interviews, let's go back to the initial example of Future Technology.

David has to interview four candidates for the junior mechanical engineer position. What steps should he take to design the most effective interview possible? First, he needs to ensure that he incorporates a level of *standardization* in his interviewing process, so that all candidates are treated in a fair and systematic way. As such, he needs to ask the same questions in the same order to Rachel, Kareem, and the other two applicants. Those questions should not be traditional questions taken from a list that applicants can prepare for; they should be job specific. David thus needs to clearly understand the unique knowledge, skills, abilities, or competencies required for the position. One pertinent approach is to engage in a job analysis process – for instance, by interrogating current job incumbents or their supervisors to discover *critical incidents* (i.e., impactful job situations) and the appropriate behaviours that competent employees are expected to demonstrate when facing them. Based on this information, David can start designing behavioural interview questions, ideally including a combination of questions asking candidates to describe how they managed similar situations in the past (i.e., *past-behavioural* questions) and how they would deal with hypothetical job-specific situations in the future (i.e., *situational* questions). David should also constitute a *panel* by inviting two other managers (ideally with diverse backgrounds) to participate in the interview. While one interviewer asks behavioural questions, another takes descriptive notes of the applicants' responses.

If applicants' responses lack details, David can follow-up using the STAR technique. Similarly, from the applicant's perspective, using the STAR technique to structure responses is recommended. It would help Rachel or Kareem to provide a more comprehensive overview of their qualifications and accomplishments as well as increase the likelihood of them being evaluated positively.

Finally, David should prepare *anchored rating scales* to help the panel evaluate applicants' answers for each question. The scales should comprise both descriptions of behaviours and examples of responses for different levels (i.e., describing very inappropriate to very appropriate behavioural responses). Interviewers can use them as benchmarks to score applicants' responses, calculate overall scores, and compare applicants to identify the most suitable for the position.

Some interviewers may (at first) be reluctant to change their interviewing habits and invest the time, money, and energy into designing such interviews.[22] They may be poorly informed about the value of behavioural approaches to interviewing.[23] But the return on investment can be very important – for instance, by ensuring higher reliability, content or predictive validity, and legal defensibility. It is also important to note that this represents a long-term investment for interviewers and their organization. Indeed, the behavioural questions and rating scales that they create can be stored in a database, which will grow every time interviewers have to design interview questions for new critical situations. When the organization needs to interview candidates for the same job or other jobs requiring similar skills or competences in the future, existing questions and scales can be used again. This is what some large organizations, like Google, have recently started to do. But correctly setting the stage for high-quality interviews is something interviewers in all organizations (both small and large) can do. Even David at Future Technology!

Toolbox

Although this Toolbox is intended primarily for interviewers, applicants can also use the example questions for interview preparation: identify what skills/competencies might be relevant for the job applied for, read the relevant questions, and practice providing responses.

Chapter 2 – Toolbox

Additional examples of past-behavioural interview questions
Initiative and citizenship:
• Tell me about a time when you had to go above and beyond the call of duty in order to get a job done. What was the situation, and what did you do? • Could you describe a situation where you proposed a new idea or initiative that benefitted the entire organization or improved the well-being of all employees? • Tell me about a time when a colleague or subordinate was in trouble, and you took it upon yourself to help them deal with the situation.
Problem-solving:
• Describe a situation where you had to solve a difficult or complex problem to move forward. What was the issue, and what did you do to resolve it? • Tell me about a difficult project where you and your team were "stuck" but you eventually found a solution to complete it. Why were you stuck, and how did you get out of or resolve the issue?

continued . . .

(Continued)

Communication:

- Tell me about a time when you had to explain something complex (for instance, a complex concept or the technical features of an object) to someone who was not familiar with it. How did you approach this situation?
- Describe a situation where you had to deliver some bad news to someone. What was the message you had to transmit? How did you approach the person(s) to explain things?

Persuasion:

- Describe a situation where you were able to successfully convince someone (or several people) to see things your way or do something that you wanted them to do.
- Please describe a time when you needed to negotiate with another person or a group who had conflicting interests. What was your approach? How did it work out?

Teamwork or collaboration:

- Tell me about a project where you had to work together with other people or as part of a team to achieve a common goal.
- Describe a time when you had to collaborate or partner with others to succeed at a task. What was the task you had to accomplish? What made the collaboration successful? What was your role or contribution?
- Please describe a time when you had to develop collaborative working relationships with colleagues from other teams or departments within your organization. How did you go about establishing and maintaining such relationships?

Leadership:

- Tell me about a situation or a project where you were in charge of managing or leading a group of people to achieve a specific objective.
- Describe a time when you took the lead on a group project. What was the project, how did you behave as a leader, and what was the outcome?
- Describe a time when your leadership was challenged. How did you respond to the situation? What was the outcome?

Decision-making:

- Describe a situation where you had to evaluate the risks, benefits, and potential outcomes associated with a decision – for instance, buying something important, investing in something, starting a new project, etc. How did you handle it?
- Tell me about a time when you had to choose among several alternatives to invest important resources (like time, money, personnel, etc.). How did you approach this situation, and what did you decide?

---

continued . . .

(Continued)

Organization or time management:
• Please tell me about a time when you had to complete a project that required you to manage and complete multiple or competing tasks, each with a tight deadline. How did you handle this situation? What steps did you take? • Please describe a situation where you had a large number of tasks to accomplish on your "to do list," but not enough time to do all of them. How did you approach the situation?
Resilience:
• Can you describe a situation where you received a negative evaluation from your supervisor (at work or in school)? What was the reason for the evaluation, and how did you handle it? • Tell me about a time when you had to keep a positive attitude when facing a difficult situation. What was your approach?

Additional examples of situational interview questions	
Competency	*Integrity*
Relevant Job(s)	*Construction Inspector*
Question	You are asked to replace a colleague who called in sick. You are instructed to inspect the recently completed installation of all of the plumbing components in a new apartment building downtown. While inspecting plumbing equipment in the basement of the building, you notice wiring coming out of a set of electrical panels. Upon closer examination, you realize that although each panel was properly installed, the way they were connected together may violate code. When you point this out to the builders, they explain that they were pressured by their client to complete the project asap and took some shortcuts. But they claim that this was already inspected and approved by your colleague a week ago, and they even show you the inspection report. What would you do in this situation?
Competency	*Initiative*

continued . . .

(Continued)

Relevant Job(s)	*Police Officer*
Question	While on your lunch break, a serious road accident involving multiple cars is reported on your radio. A team from a different location can reach the accident site, but it will take them at least an hour to arrive. When you arrive at the location, you observe three heavily damaged vehicles, with the possibility of injured victims in all three cars. Other emergency professionals, such as EMTs or firefighters, are not yet on the scene. A crowd of curious bystanders starts to converge around the accident, while traffic also starts to accumulate. Your team consists of only three people, including yourself. How would you approach this situation?
Competency	*Teamwork*
Relevant Job(s)	*Accountant or Auditor*
Question	You have been working together with four colleagues on an audit for the past month. You have just one week before your report is due and a lot of tasks to finish. In the past few days, two of your team members have started to argue about the best way to reconcile the expenses on a number of accounts. This morning the debate turned into a heated argument, with the two colleagues insulting one another. Now both refuse to work with each other, and one even left for lunch break and did not come back. What would you do to manage this situation and ensure that the report deadline is met?
Competency	*Decision-making*
Relevant Job(s)	*Technician in the electricity sector*
Question	You are working with a long-time colleague to repair a power line. Suddenly, he makes a small mistake and gets a severe electric shock. The colleague tells you that he is feeling OK and asks you not to tell anyone, especially not your supervisor, as he is afraid of getting in trouble for not following proper procedures. This would violate the company protocol.

continued . . .

(Continued)

	But he tells you that he was previously warned by your boss that mistakes like this might cost him his job. How would you react?
Competency	*Communication*
Relevant Job(s)	*Sales Associate in an electronics store*
Question	Imagine that you are working in the television department of a local electronics store. It is a busy Saturday afternoon on the last weekend before Christmas, and a 70-year-old lady approaches you. She would like to buy a new TV as a gift for her 20-year-old grandson, but she is not sure what model she should buy. She is especially confused about the differences between LED and Plasma TVs as well as between Full-HD and 4K TVs. What would you do?
Competency	*Organization*
Relevant Job(s)	*Management position in the retail sector*
Question	Imagine that you are the assistant store manager. The store manager is away for training and left you in charge. It is Saturday morning. Three cashiers have called in sick for the day. A new hire working in inventory is here for her first day and should receive training. A line is forming at the customer service desk, and customers are asking to talk to a manager. You have to finalize accounting tasks for the month and send your report to company headquarters by the end of the day. What steps would you take to respond to the situations you are currently facing?
Competency	*Prioritization*
Relevant Job(s)	*Operations Manager in the financial sector*
Question	During your first week on the job, you find out that before your arrival the Operations Manager's responsibilities were divided among several other department heads and members of upper management. With you now on the team, the other staff have started offloading operational tasks and unfinished projects to you. You already have five ongoing projects, and each requires about four or five hours of work to be completed, including two projects

continued . . .

(Continued)

	with deadlines by the end of the week. Today your boss gives you a new project, which is described as "important." On top of this, you are still in the process of familiarizing yourself with the company's financial reporting systems, company policies, etc. How would you proceed?
Competency	*Delegation*
Relevant Job(s)	*Business Consultant*
Question	A team that you oversee has to develop a leadership training program for a client. You have three consultants on the team. There are two senior consultants who have extensive experience in delivering such programs, but they are also involved with other projects. There is one junior consultant who is willing to work very hard, but whose experience and capabilities in this area are limited. This is a very important project, and your team is under time pressure from the client. How would you allocate work between the three consultants?

Notes

1 Cook, K., *65 interview questions: Conquer your fear and answer the toughest job interview questions*. 2008, Southfield, MI: Equity Press.
2 Chen, C.-H.V., H.-M. Lee, and Y.-J.Y. Yeh, *The antecedent and consequence of person-organization fit: Ingratiation, similarity, hiring recommendations and job offer*. International Journal of Selection and Assessment, 2008. **16**: p. 210–219.
3 Tsai, W.-C., et al., *Disentangling the effects of applicant defensive impression management tactics in job interviews*. International Journal of Selection and Assessment, 2010. **18**: p. 131–140.
4 Levashina, J., et al., *The structured employment interview: Narrative and quantitative review of the research literature*. Personnel Psychology, 2014. **67**(1): p. 241–293.
5 Kepes, S., et al., *Publication bias in the organizational sciences*. Organizational Research Methods, 2012. **15**(4): p. 624–662.
6 Lievens, F., and A. De Paepe, *An empirical investigation of interviewer-related factors that discourage the use of high structure interviews*. Journal of Organizational Behavior, 2004. **25**: p. 29–46.

7   Williamson, L.G., et al., *Employment interview on trial: Linking interview structure with litigation outcomes*. Journal of Applied Psychology, 1997. **82**(6): p. 900–912.

8   Roth, P.L., and J.E. Campion, *An analysis of the predictive power of the panel interview and pre-employment tests*. Journal of Occupational and Organizational Psychology, 1992. **65**(1): p. 51–60.

9   Campion, M.A., D.K. Palmer, and J.E. Campion, *A review of structure in the selection interview*. Personnel Psychology, 1997. **50**: p. 655–702.

10 Latham, G.P., and D.P. Skarlicki, *The effectiveness of situational, patterned behaviour, and conventional structured interview in minimising in-group favouritism of Canadian francophone managers*. Applied Psychology: An International Review, 1996. **45**(2): p. 177–184.

11 Janz, T., *Initial comparisons of patterned behavior description interviews versus unstructured interviews*. Journal of Applied Psychology, 1982. **67**: p. 577–580; Latham, G.P., et al., *The situational interview*. Journal of Applied Psychology, 1980. **64**(4): p. 422–427.

12 Sanchez, J.I., and E.L. Levine, *What is (or should be) the difference between competency modeling and traditional job analysis?* Human Resource Management Review, 2009. **19**(2): p. 53–63.

13 Levashina, J., et al., *The structured employment interview: Narrative and quantitative review of the research literature*. Personnel Psychology, 2014. **67**(1): p. 241–293.

14 Bangerter, A., P. Corvalan, and C. Cavin, *Storytelling in the selection interview?: How applicants respond to past behavior questions*. Journal of Business and Psychology, 2014. **29**(4): p. 593–604.

15 Tross, S.A., and T.J. Maurer, *The effect of coaching interviewees on subsequent interview performance in structured experience-based interviews*. Journal of Occupational and Organizational Psychology, 2008. **81**: p. 589–605.

16 Levashina, J., et al., *The structured employment interview: Narrative and quantitative review of the research literature*. Personnel Psychology, 2014. **67**(1): p. 241–293.

17 Latham, G.P., et al., *The situational interview*. Journal of Applied Psychology, 1980. **64**(4): p. 422–427.

18 Decety, J., et al., *Vegetative response during imagined movement is proportional to mental effort*. Behavioural Brain Research, 1991. **42**: p. 1–5.

19 Latham, G.P., and C. Sue-Chan, *A meta-analysis of the situational interview: An enumerative review of reasons for its validity*. Canadian Psychology, 1999. **40**(1): p. 56–67.

20 Levashina, J., et al., *The structured employment interview: Narrative and quantitative review of the research literature*. Personnel Psychology, 2014. **67**(1): p. 241–293.

21 Melchers, K.G., et al., *Is more structure really better?: A comparison of frame-of-reference training and descriptively-anchored rating scales to improve interviewers' rating quality*. Personnel Psychology, 2011. **64**(1): p. 53–87.

22 Lievens, F., and A. De Paepe, *An empirical investigation of interviewer-related factors that discourage the use of high structure interviews.* Journal of Organizational Behavior, 2004. **25**: p. 29–46.
23 Roulin, N., and A. Bangerter, *Understanding the academic-practitioner gap for structured interviews: "Behavioral" interviews diffuse, "structured" interviews do not.* International Journal of Selection and Assessment, 2012. **20**(2): p. 149–158.

Let the show begin

How to interview effectively from both sides of the table

Job interviews as social interactions

Rachel and Kareem, our two young engineers on the job market, are both scheduled to interview tomorrow for a position at Brilliant Electronics, a multinational company specializing in smartphone technology. The HR manager at Brilliant Electronics, Alice, has designed a standardized interview with a set of job-related behavioural questions that she plans to use for all candidates. Alice thus appears to rely on the effective interview techniques (instead of poorly-designed interviews) that I highlighted in the last chapter, thus increasing the likelihood of making an optimal hiring decision. "What could go wrong?" you may ask.

Well, a lot of things actually! Indeed, the quality of the interviewing process (and, ultimately, the hiring decisions) will also depend on how the applicant and the interviewer behave or perform. Give a Stradivarius violin and Mozart's Symphony Number 40 score to a gifted and trained violonist, and you may enjoy a lovely concert. Give the same instruments to your five-year-old nephew who never played music, and it

DOI: 10.4324/9781003171089-3

is likely to be a disaster. Similarly, the interview is only an instrument, and even the best instruments require applicants and interviewers to be prepared and able to perform to be truly effective.

Although a large portion of the existing research has focused on designing job interviews that are more efficient (i.e, more valid and more reliable predictors of future job performance), we should not forget that the interview is, at its core, a social interaction between two (or more) individuals.[1] Applicants and interviewers arrive with their own objectives, doubts, expectations, attitudes, and preferences regarding the interview, which will likely influence how they behave. In this chapter, I describe both applicants' and interviewers' behaviours during the interview, and how they may (positively or negatively) impact interview outcomes. I will also emphasize potential cultural factors (or international differences in interviewing practices) that can impact interview effectiveness around the world.

Effective interviewing for job applicants

Applicants are usually depicted as being in the most difficult position in the job interview. Their responses and behaviours are judged by the interviewer (or a group of interviewers), and they have to perform in order to convince the interviewer(s) that they are the right person for the job. As such, interviews are associated with a number of emotional or cognitive reactions for applicants, who have to cope with anxiety, appropriately prepare themselves, manage their expectations, and try to understand what the interviewer is trying to assess in order to succeed. Relying on research findings on interview anxiety, preparation or training, expectations, and the ability to identify selection criteria, I illustrate below what Rachel and Kareem can do to improve their performance in interviews.

Dealing with interview anxiety

As described above, the job interview is a social interaction, which in itself can be stressful for some people. Moreover, it is also quite unique, because the applicant's performance is judged by the interviewer (or interviewers). As such, interviews are likely to create anxiety for applicants like Kareem. Although interview anxiety is often associated with observable behaviours, such as weak knees, shaking hands, or sweaty palms, it can take a number of other (less visible) forms.[2] For instance, applicants can experience communication anxiety and will be unsure of their communication skills or feel nervous about expressing their thoughts clearly to the interviewer. They can also worry about their appearance, believing that they made critical mistakes in the way they dressed, their hairstyle, or their make-up that will cost them the job. They can also be concerned about being perceived as someone who is socially inappropriate or even akward by the interviewer. Or, they may worry that they will simply be unable to perform as well as other applicants for the position.

Box 3.1

Kareem enters Alice's office and shakes her hand. While sitting on the chair in front of him, he realizes how sweaty his palm is and how soft his handshake was. Memories of his last (and likely unsuccessful) interview at Future Technology rush into his mind. Kareem really wants the job at Brilliant Electronics and knows that he has to impress Alice, but he worries that he will not be good enough to make the cut. What questions is she going to ask him? What if his answers are not clear or convincing enough? Should he talk about his passion for robot competitions or not (remember, this topic did not work very well last time)? Does the colour of his tie match his shirt?

Interview anxiety can take many forms, but can also be difficult to spot for an interviewer. For instance, one may believe that applicants who are more anxious will display a number of cues or non-verbal behaviours that make anxiety visible. We all have in mind scenes, likely from movies or TV shows, in which the main characters cannot control their stress and start fidgeting, moving their bodies or hands, nodding repeatedly, speaking too fast, or attempting to avoid eye contact as much as possible. However, research suggests that such behaviours are often *not* associated with applicant anxiety in interviews.[3] On the contrary, anxious applicants tend to engage slightly *less* in those behaviours: they nod less, engage in less hand movement, and speak more slowly! As such, even if interviewers are trying to assess when applicants are anxious – for instance, to help them feel more comfortable – it would be very difficult to do so.

Of practical importance for job candidates like Kareem (and Rachel), anxiety can have destructive effects on their performance during the interview. Anxious applicants are perceived less positively by evaluators. For instance, they are seen as being less confident, less enthusiastic, less likeable, or less professional, all traits that are usually valued by organizations.[4] And, such perceptions are likely to impact interviewers' evaluations of applicants' suitability for the position: the more anxious applicants are during the interview, the lower their performance ratings will be.[5] It is likely that some applicants are anxious because they are not fully qualified for the position they applied for. In that case, the anxiety is actually helpful (at least from the perspective of the hiring organization), because it reduces the chances that an unqualified applicant will get the job. Yet, it is also possible that some highly qualified candidates will experience anxiety, which may reduce their chances of impressing the interviewer and getting the job. Overall, research shows that applicants who experience more anxiety during a job interview (and are thus evaluated more negatively by interviewers) do not necessarily end up being poorer performers at work.[6] As such, applicant anxiety could reduce the validity of the interview – that is, it could hinder its effectiveness in helping interviewers select the most qualified applicants. Taking the organizations' perspective, it is therefore possible to overlook some top candidates because anxiety prevented them from performing at their best.

Interestingly, although female applicants tend to experience more anxiety than their male counterparts, male applicants tend to be less effective in managing their anxiety, and it is mostly males' interview performance that suffers.[7] In other words, Rachel is likely to feel more stressed during her interview than Kareem. Yet, Kareem's anxiety is more likely to negatively impact his performance, whereas Rachel will likely be better able to cope with the anxiety. Rachel and (especially) Kareem would thus benefit from engaging in training or preparation strategies to reduce (or at least manage) their anxiety in future job interviews.

Let's go back in time and imagine that Kareem and Rachel still have a full day (or more) before their interview at Brilliant Electronics. What can they do to manage anxiety and, more generally, ensure that they enter the interview room ready to make the best impression possible? If they experience high levels of anxiety in various forms of social situations (or what psychologists sometimes refer to *trait* anxiety), one day of preparation will likely not be enough. Such forms of anxiety may require counseling or interventions using clinical psychology techniques and the help of a therapist (e.g., relaxation training, mindfullness, cognitive behavioural therapy), which are beyond the scope of the present book. However, if candidates are specifically anxious during job interviews or some specific interviews (i.e., *state* anxiety), then short-term preparation or training strategies can be effective.

As mentioned above, female applicants tend to use better coping strategies to manage anxiety. But what do these strategies look like in practice? Psychology research suggests that only emotion-oriented and problem-oriented coping strategies are effective, whereas other (e.g., avoidance-oriented) strategies are less effective.[8] Emotion coping is an affect-based strategy that involves sharing one's anxiety with others, such as friends or family members, before the event (i.e., the interview). By doing so, the applicant can regulate their emotional reactions toward the stressful event (i.e., the interview) and alleviate the impact it may have on their performance. Alternatively, problem-oriented coping is a task-based strategy that requires developing plans of action, such as using breathing techniques or rehearsed responses to interview questions, to handle anxiety when it arises during the interview.[9] Rachel and (especially) Kareem may thus benefit from using those two coping strategies to manage their anxiety about upcoming interviews – that is, talking to their friends and preparing themselves.

Preparation and training

Psychology research has examined how applicants can prepare for upcoming interviews. As described above, such preparation can be a strategy to cope with interview anxiety, but it is also a valuable approach even for very confident candidates. The initial preparation stage involves gathering information about job interviews in general or about the organization they will be interviewing with. For instance, applicants can accumulate information about how job interviews are usually conducted, what questions they can expect, or even how to answer them by reading *how-to* or *advice* books or by visiting specialized websites. Such a strategy helps candidates reduce their uncertainty about the interview (i.e., Kareem worrying about the questions that he would be asked) and replace it with actual interview-related knowledge.[10] However, not all sources of information aimed at helping applicants prepare should be considered equivalent.[11] Some books or websites will provide applicants with specific advice to *beat* the interviewer (or organization), such as ready-to-use answers to typical or popular questions. Although this can certainly reduce applicants' anxiety, such books only help applicants prepare for a small number of specific interview questions. In addition, the risk with this approach is that it can motivate applicants to provide falisifed information to interviewers. As such, it may creates *false positives* – that is, situations where underqualified applicants get jobs they do not deserve. Imagine that Stephan applies for the engineer job at Brilliant Electronics. He is largely unqualified compared to candidates like Kareem or Rachel, but he is able to get an interview by exaggerating on his resume. Stephan spends hours preparing for the interview, reading every book or visiting every website he can find, and rehearsing answers to questions that he expects to be asked during the interview (based on the ready-to-use advice he found and not his actual experiences). If he is evaluated more positively than Kareem and Rachel (who may have underperformed because of anxiety, for instance), his preparation strategy has created a *false positive*: he may be hired instead of objectively better-fitted candidates! That being said, remember that if the organization uses behavioural interviews (as presented in Chapter 2), the *false positive* cases are less likely to occur because such questions are more difficult for unqualified applicants to anticipate and prepare for.

Alternatively, other books or websites will help applicants understand the goals, mechanisms, and features of job interviews.[12] For instance, they may describe how behavioural interview questions work and thus encourage applicants to anticipate potential questions, think about past experiences that would be pertinent for such questions, and ultimately arrive at the interview with a set of narratives to tell the interviewer based on those experiences. (This is the approach this very chapter – and book – is following!) Such a prepation approach does not tell applicants what they should do or say (nor does it enourage deception). Instead, it helps them to explore their own past, identify relevant situations they faced, and highlight their responses to the situations.

In order find the most relevant past experiences, applicants would also benefit from gathering additional information about the job and the organization. Kareem only needs a computer or a smartphone with internet access and a few minutes to obtain valuable data through a search engine or from the Brilliant Eletronics website and social media pages. Within this type of preparation, applicants can also engage in *mental imagery*. This technique involves mentally recreating past work experiences, visualizing how they performed in those situations, and using this mental representation to build effective responses for the upcoming interview (see also the "Toolbox" at the end of this chapter). The technique can help candidates to reduce their stress and improve their performance during the interview.[13] Altogether, this type of preparation inspires candidates to provide honest and insighful responses to interviewers' questions. It is beneficial to both the applicant (who is less anxious and can perform better during the interview) and the organization (that can gather more vaulable information about the applicant to make a valid decision).

An alternative to individual preparation or self-study is for applicants to participate in training or coaching sessions. For young graduates like Kareem and Rachel, such sessions are often provided by the career centers of their college or university. Unemployed individuals may sometimes take advantage of similar training sessions through employment agencies and governmental services. Finally, training sessions are also offered by private organizations or consultants. If such coaching sessions are well designed, there is evidence that they can help improve applicants' performance in subsequent interviews. For instance, in one study, a number of police officers and firefighters were interviewing to get a promotion. A group of them were provided with a brief (1.5- to 2-hour) coaching session, which included information about standardized interview formats, advice about appropriate behaviours, and a role-play. As compared to a non-coached group, those who were provided with coaching performed significantly better in their interviews.[14] Training and coaching sessions can also provide candidates with tips regarding how to behave during the interview. For instance, research suggests that the quality of the handshake exchanged with the interviewer at the beginning of the interview can influence performance evaluations.[15] Candidates can thus learn how to perform a "good" handshake – that is, use a strong and complete grip, shake vigorously for a lasting duration, and make eye contact while hands are clasped. Importantly for organizations, if coaching sessions are oriented towards helping candidates to focus on and convey job-relevant information in their responses, they can actually increase the validity of the interviewing process. In other words, ensuring that applicants are provided with information and coaching about behavioural questions and the expected form of responses will make interviews *better* predictors of future job performance.[16]

Identifying the selection criteria

In the previous section, I highlighted that applicants should prepare for interviews by trying to identify what qualities the organization is looking for, considering past experiences where they used such qualities, and preparing a set of narratives to tell the interviewer. This approach is also associated with the concept of applicants' *ability to identify the criteria* used by an organization (or *ATIC*).[17] Note that the ATIC concept is not limited to the interview, but also applies to other selection situations, such as personality tests or assessment center exercises. The concept of ATIC captures individuals' ability to read situational cues in order to discover what skills or competencies the organization (or interviewer) is trying to assess. These cues can be gathered by the applicant during the selection process. For instance, the candidate listens to an interview question and attempts to identify what skill, ability, competency, or specific behaviour the question is assessing. But applicants can also anticipate questions prior to the interview – for example, by analyzing the job advertisement or description to identify key requirements. Or, they can review information published by the employer (e.g., on the company's website, in brochures, or provided to the applicant via email) to discover what attitudes or values are particularly important or recognized in the organization. Research shows that some applicants are better than others at this identification task (i.e., have higher ATIC scores). Moreover, high-ATIC individuals can then use the information they have gathered to adapt their behaviour to better match the organization's expectations, and thus increase their performance in the interview.[18]

Box 3.2

Imagine that Alice asks Rachel and Kareem the following question: "Tell me about a time when you had to explain something complex to someone who was not familiar with it." This question was designed to assess a specific competency (i.e., communication). If Rachel can identify that the question is about communication (i.e., if she demonstrates high ATIC), she is more likely to provide a relevant answer. For instance, she could rely on a professional past experience and describe how she successfully explained the complex mechanisms of a machine to a manager during an internship. Or, she could recall a personal experience and describe how she effectively explained the technical features of a smartphone to her grandmother. Such a response will likely reflect what Alice expected to learn about Rachel's qualities or behaviours, and thus it may be positively evaluated. However, if Kareem fails to correctly identify the criteria attached to this question (and thus demonstrates lower ATIC) – for instance, if he believes that the question is about persuasion – he may discuss an experience that is less relevant. For example, he may describe a time when he convinced a customer to purchase a high-end product that the customer did not need. Such a response may thus lead to a lower evaluation from Alice, because Kareem failed to directly demonstrate the communication skills that she expected to learn about.

What is the actual impact of ATIC for job candidates and hiring organizations? Overall, empirical research highlights that ATIC can be beneficial for both parties.[19] For applicants, the ability to identify criteria is positively related to performance during the interview. The relationship between ATIC and interview performance is also stronger when applicants are behaving honestly rather than when they are instructed to "put their best foot forward," which suggests that it is associated with individuals' truthful qualities.[20] Importantly, indviduals high in ATIC are also likely to perform better on the job, suggesting that ATIC does not simply help applicants to succeed at the interview, but also possesses some predictive validity. There are two psychological explanations for this. First, the ATIC-job performance relationship is partly due to the conceptual similarity between ATIC and cognitive ability (i.e., a form of intelligence). Indeed, job applicants with higher cognitive abilities are better at identifying selection criteria. And, we also know from industrial psychology research that individuals with higher cognitive abilities are (in general) better performers at work.[21] Therefore, higher ATIC should be indirectly associated with higher job performance as well. Second, ATIC can be seen as a form of social competence that helps individuals analyze and respond to ambiguous situations. If applicants are able to correctly identify what is expected of them during an interview, they may be able to deal with similarly ambiguous situations at work. For instance, high-ATIC people may know how to react when their boss provides unclear instructions to perform a task.

Based on the example provided above, Alice may have two good reasons to value Rachel (over Kareem) as an applicant for the Brilliant Electronics job. If Rachel can identify what the interview questions are assessing, she is probably quite intelligent and capable of handling uncertainty at work – two qualities that Alice should value. That said, there is some research showing that making job interviews more transparent by revealing the skills or competencies that will be evaluated in the interview can be beneficial too. For instance, a series of studies compared interviews where some applicants were told that the questions would be assessing skills like leadership, planning, or cooperation, whereas other applicants were not.[22] Those in the transparent interviews performed better.

Importantly for organizations, both transparent and non-transparent interviews were similarly predictive of subsequent performance in work-like simulations. In other words, it would be possible for Alice to "level the playing field" by providing all candidates with the same information about what the interview will be assessing. Doing so would eliminate differences in ATIC between Rachel and Kareem, and thus both applicants would be given the same chances to perform. For instance, Kareem would be told that the question "Tell me about a time when you had to explain something complex to someone who was not familiar with it" is evaluating communication (not persuasion), thus he could provide Alice a better answer. This might increase the fairness of the interview (at least from Kareem's point of view). In addition, it would still ensure a valid process, although it would prevent Rachel from using her higher ATIC level (which could be a job-relevant ability that Alice might want to know about and value).

Managing pre-interview expectations

Job applicants also usually go to an interview with a set of expectations, which can impact how they behave and perform during the interview and influence various interview outcomes. As such, it is important that both candidates and interviewers understand those expectations and manage them effectively. Research suggests that applicants form expectations about five key aspects of job interviews.[23] First, they expect to be treated with warmth and respect by the interviewer. Second, they expect the interview to be designed and conducted in a way that offers them opportunities to demonstrate their qualities and their potential to the organization. Third, they expect that only qualified individuals should be hired, and that it would be difficult for unqualified applicants to succeed by simply pretending to possess the necessary qualities. Fourth, applicants expect the assessment of their qualifications to be done in a fair and unbiased way. Fifth and finally, they expect the organization to inform them about their performance during the interview.

Those expectations are practically important, because they serve as anchors for applicants' post-interview perceptions.[24] For instance, how warm and respectful a candidate expects the interviewer to be prior to the interview will be strongly related to how they actually perceived the interviewer to act after the interview. If they expected the interviewer to be cold and disrespectful, they are more likely to view him or her as behaving accordingly (even if the interviewer actually behaved in a warm and respectful way). Job applicants thus engage in what psychology researchers have called *confirmatory processes* – that is, what happens during the interview is seen through the lens of their pre-interview expectations. This can be problematic if the lens is defective. Indeed, if applicants' expectations are initially biased (e.g., under- or over-estimated), their reactions to the interview will also be biased. But expectations do not only influence perceptions, they can also affect how applicants' behave during the interview or react to it.[25] For instance, applicants who expect unfair or disrespectful treatment will be more anxious, less motivated, and more likely to underperform in the interview. Indeed, why would they bother doing their best if they think that the outcome will be unfair to them anyway? But having (too) high expectations can also be counterproductive. Applicants who arrive at the interview with high expectations but then are treated less fairly than expected will experience a *reality shock*, which will create negative affect (e.g., getting frustrated) and psychological withdrawal (e.g., losing interest in the interview or the job).

Furthermore, applicants' initial expectations can indirectly influence important interview outcomes.[26] For instance, candidates' expectations regarding being treated with warmth and respect can ultimately impact their attraction to the organization or their intention to recommend the organization. As such, if Kareem arrives at Brilliant Electronics expecting Alice to be warm and respectful, he is more likely to actually see Alice as demonstrating those positive attitudes during the interview, which will confirm his attraction to the company and make him more likely to tell his friends to apply there too. Alternatively, if Rachel arrives at Brilliant Electronics expecting Alice to be cold and disrespectful, she is more likely to perceive Alice as being unfriendly and harsh during the interview, which will reduce her attraction to the company and make her more likely to discourage her friends from applying there.

Altogether, both job applicants and organizations would benefit from having more realistic pre-interview expectations. It is therefore important for applicants to be able to effectively set and manage their expectations, but also for organizations to help them in that endeavour. For applicants, expectations can be adjusted by collecting more information about the organization and the selection process – for instance, by visiting the organization's website, reading available documents, performing online searches, or speaking with friends or colleagues who have experience with the organization.[27] Organizations are also responsible for providing enough (and realistic) information to candidates – for instance, before the interview explaining the various steps of the selection process or how decisions are made. Initial interactions between the interviewer and applicants (e.g., via an email or quick phone call) might also help form more accurate expectations.

Effective interviewing for interviewers

The first part of this chapter shed some light on the factors that may impact applicants' interview performance and how to manage them. For instance, I described ways that applicants can deal with interview anxiety, prepare themselves, identify the selection criteria, and manage their expectations to perform at their best. Yet, a successful interview also requires interviewers to behave appropriately and respectfully, as well as ensure that the interviewing process remains fair and unbiased. As such, I highlight below what interviewers like Alice can do to ensure that all applicants are placed in optimal performance conditions. I also describe behaviours that promote fairness in the process and result in positive reactions from applicants.

Understanding applicants' reactions

Organizations and interviewers should ensure that they rely on a reliable and valid interview process to make optimal hiring decisions. However, it is important to acknowledge that the interview serves two functions. One the one hand, it allows interviewers to gather information about applicants to make a decision about their suitability for the job. On the other hand, it also allows applicants to form a more precise impression about the organization (and the job) and confirm that it is really where they want to work. Therefore, interviewers must make sure that applicants leave the interview with positive impressions or reactions. How applicants view the interview (and, more generally, the selection) process can impact how much effort they invest when interviewing.[28] In other words, applicants who feel poorly treated might be less motivated to do their best in the interview. As a result, interviewers might evaluate them less positively and possibly miss out on very qualified candidates for the position.

Applicants' reactions can also have a major influence on acceptance rates. Applicants who have negative reactions are less likely accept a job offer.[29] This means that the organization may have invested substantial time and resources into identifying the ideal candidate(s) only to see them reject an offer. But the negative impact of applicants' reactions can go beyond the decision of one isolated candidate and impact the organization's wider public image as a potential employer through word-of-mouth.[30] For instance, research suggests that disappointed candidates may share their experience with the friends, colleagues, or family members, who may in turn view the organization as being less attractive. If this was perhaps a minor issue for organizations ten or twenty years ago, it can become a major problem today. Why? Because the internet and social media have made people much more interconnected, and information is easier to share.

Imagine that Rachel leaves Brilliant Electronics with a negative impression. She is unhappy with her interaction with Alice, the questions she was asked during the interview, or the way the whole process was managed by the organization. She returns home certain that she does not want to work for Brilliant Electronics. This is perhaps a loss for the company, if Rachel was rated as the best candidate by Alice. A few years ago, Rachel may have only talked to a few close friends about it. But today she is likely to share her impressions online with her entire network. Her Facebook friends and Twitter or Instagram followers will know about it. This may represent dozens (or, in extreme cases, hundreds or thousands) of people – but those individuals may also decide to share Rachel's negative experience with their own networks. In a few hours, due to the kind of rapid snowball effect faciliated by social media, a very large number of individuals will have heard of it. In the worst case scenario, Rachel's story could become viral and touch hundreds of thousands. Of course, not all of them are potential applicants for Brilliant Electronics, but the impact on the organization's reputation can be important. Rachel could also share her experience on websites specifically designed to review employers (e.g., Glassdoor) or on plaforms where people share their experiences (e.g., Reddit). In some cases, job applicants are also organizations' regular customers, and negative selection experiences could influence their fidelity to the company's products or brands.[31]

We should not forget that similar effects can emerge when applicants have positive reactions. For instance, Kareem may have a wonderful experience interviewing with Alice, share it with his network, and indirectly motivate other people to apply to the organization. Yet, we know from years of research in psychology, communication, and marketing that negative stories are much more likely to be shared, both through word-of-mouth and social media, than positive stories. It is therefore imperative that organizations and interviewers ensure that applicants' reactions are as positive as possible.

In recent decades, industrial psychology researchers have examined applicants' reactions to a number of different selection methods as well as how technology and individual or cultural characteristics can influence reactions. Job interviews are generally associated with positive reactions. In research summarizing the results of multiple studies conducted across 17 countries, the interview was consistently ranked the second most preferred selection method (just behind work sample tests) in all countries.[32] Applicants perceived interviews more favourably than other selection techniques, such as cognitive ability, personality, or integrity tests. Interviews are also rated very favourably in terms of employers' rights to use, opportunity to perform, and face validity. In other words, applicants believe that organizations should use interviews to assess them, interviews usually offer enough opportunities to demonstrate candidates' qualities to interviewers, and interviews are valid predictors of future job performance. Moreover, because it is one of the only face-to-face selection methods, interviews are also perceived to be "warmer" than other selection techniques (but see also the discussion of technology-mediated interviews in Chapter 5).

A key factor in positive reactions is how fair candidates perceive the interviewing process to be. Job applicants attach a great deal of importance to the fairness of the selection process and to the interview in particular. Researchers have argued that a fair process involves high levels of *procedural* and *distributive* justice.[33] An interview will be evaluated as being high in *procedural* justice if it is administred in a consistent manner, if the questions are perceived to be relevant for the job, if applicants are given enough opportunities and provided with enough information to demonstrate their qualities, or if applicants are provided with feedback on their performance. Moreover, an interview will be evaluated as being high in *distributive* justice if the evaluation and, ultimately, the hiring decision are perceived to fair, unbiased, and consistent with applicants' efforts or performance. In other words, the interview would be seen as just if applicants think that they got the outcome that they deserved. But it would be seen as unjust if they estimate that someone less deserving was hired for the job instead.

Yet, not all interviews will lead to positive reactions. Interviews that are more standardized (or more structured) are usually perceived as being more difficult, and they can be perceived more negatively by job applicants than more traditional or unstructured interviews.[34] This highlights a particularly interesting paradox for interviewers. As described in Chapter 2, interviews that are more standardized and rely on behavioural questions are objectively better. They allow employers to assess candidates more thoroughly and reliably as well as better predict the likelihood that applicants will be high performers if hired. Theoretically, highly structured interviews are more aligned with most of the elements of procedural and distributive justice described above. However, job applicants tend to react more positively to less structured or standardized interview formats, which are actually less valid. Although psychology research has yet to find an ideal combination of interview features that ensure both effective hiring decisions and positive applicant reactions, two cautious recommendations can be offered. First, interviewers should clearly explain the features, purposes, and advantages of the chosen interviewing technique to applicants. For instance, Alice should tell candidates at the beginning of the interview that she will ask questions about past experiences or rely on hypothetical scenarios to assess qualifications that are essential for the job. Second, applicants should be provided with some guidance on how to formulate their answers, either by the interviewer at the beginning of the interview or in advance of the meeting. The discussion of interview transparancy in the previous section is a relevant example. Alternatively, Alice could encourage candidates to answer questions about their past experiences using the situation-task-action-result (STAR) method described in Chapter 2 (see also the "Toolbox" at the end of this chapter).

In addition, research also suggests that providing applicants with performance feedback after practice interviews can also be beneficial.[35] Constructive feedback seems to help applicants feel more competent and confident about their interviewing skills and makes them more optimistic about the outcome of future (real) interviews. Of course, this is not something hiring managers like Alice can do to help candidates like Rachel or Kareem when they are currently interviewing for a position. Yet, if they do not get the job at Brilliant Electronics, constructive feedback might help them in future interviews (but see also the next section about how to communicate rejections to applicants). Perhaps, more importantly, it represents valuable advice for professionals whose roles involve helping job seekers prepare for interviews – for instance, those in charge of career centers at universities or colleges, employment agencies, or immigration services.

Respectfully dealing with rejected applicants

Organizations may sometimes choose to focus all of their efforts on communicating with successful applicants – that is, those who performed well during the interview and are still being considered for the position. This is certainly pertinent from a short-term recruitment perspective, because the key objective is to convince the best candidate(s) to accept a job offer. However, as illustrated with the social media example above, rejected applicants should not be overlooked. Let's imagine that Alice, the HR manager for Brilliant Electronics, was not impressed by Kareem and Rachel during their respective interviews. Should she tell them that they did not make the cut? And, if so, what is the best way for her to communicate this decision? Should she simply state that they have not been selected for the job, or should she provide a detailed explaination to justify her decision? Intuitively, one may believe that rejected applicants would like to know if and why they did not succeed. Yet, industrial psychology research suggests that the way applicants react to rejection is actually more complex.

As highlighted earlier in the chapter, applicants generally expect to be informed of the hiring decision. Moreover, when they are informed, applicants use this information to assess whether or not they believe the organization fulfilled its obligations towards them. From that point of view, an interviewer who fails to communicate a rejection decision may be seen as failing to fulfill the organization's obligations. For instance, a study compared the reactions of three groups of applicants: those who were still considered for the position, those who were informed by the organization that they had been rejected, and those who were rejected but never received any information from the organization.[36] It was mostly those applicants who were rejected without any communication who perceived the organization more negatively. They thought that the organization failed to fulfill its obligations and were less likely to reapply there in the future. However, those who were informed about the rejection decision did not have particularly negative views of the hiring organization. We thus have the first part of the answer: Alice should definitely inform candidates like Kareem and Rachel that their interviews at Brilliant Electronics were unsuccessful.

However, there is more to the story. Information about a rejection decision can tigger two types of reactions from applicants. On the one hand, they will assess the fairness of the interviewing process and the value of the organization as an employer. On the other hand, they will use the hiring organization's assessment of their qualities or qualifications to adapt their self-evaluations. Looking at applicants' reactions towards the organization, research suggests that providing explanations helps increase fairness perceptions.[37] As such, if Alice explains to Kareem and Rachel why they did not make the cut and provides feedback on their interview performance, our two candidates are likely to perceive the selection process as more fair and Brilliant Electronics as a better employer.

That being said, applicants are also likely to use feedback information to re-evaluate their self-worth or self-esteem. Individuals who are less optimistic in nature are particularly prone to being hurt by negative feedback and having their well-being or sense of self-worth negatively impacted.[38] For instance, if Alice tells Kareem that he has been rejected, his reaction could involve thoughts like, "My performance in the interview was insufficient" or "Maybe I am not good enough." Alternatively, candidates can engage in psychological processes to protect themselves – for instance, blaming the organization, the interviewer, or other external factors. Such processes are especially used by individuals who tend to attribute failures in their lives to external factors (what psychology researchers call an *external locus of control*). For instance, if Alice tells Rachel that she has been rejected, her thoughts may include "They did a poor job interviewing me" or "Maybe another applicant was much more experienced than me." Yet, the more precise the justification for the rejection is, the more difficult it is to blame external factors, even for very optimistic individuals. If Alice tells Rachel and Kareem that they do not possess the right qualifications for the job – for instance, by explaining that they are lacking analytical or problem solving skills – it may be difficult for our two candidates to blame the organization, Alice, or other candidates.

Indeed, a study compared the reactions of two groups of job applicants. The first group was provided a short standardized rejection message explaining that their score was below the selection threshold, whereas the second group received more extensive feedback on their performance during the selection process.[39] The reactions were more *negative* in the second group. More precisely, applicants who received detailed feedback after rejection experienced more negative emotions and reported lower confidence in their abilities than those who did not receive detailed feedback. We thus have the second part of the answer: Alice should probably provide Kareem and Rachel with explanations for why their interviews at Brilliant Electronics was unsuccessful. Yet, she should make sure to highlight the process used to reach the decision, not the weaknesses of the candidates.

Effective interviewing around the world

So far, I have described interviewing (best) practices independantly of the region, country, or culture in which the interview takes place. Yet, in today's globalized world it is quite likely that Rachel and Kareem will end up in an interviewing context that somehow differs from their own culture. They can decide to apply for jobs in organizations in other countries. Or they might apply for a local job in a multinational corporation headquartered in another country, which may lean towards standardized interviewing practices aligned with the company's home country. Finally, they may simply face an interviewer who is from another country or culture. Should Rachel and Kareem expect the interview to be different from their past *local* experiences? There are two main reasons why such differences may be observed. First, there are some important cultural differences, but also country-level norms, that influence interviewing practices around the world. Second, there are also differences in legislation, which can impact how interviews are designed and conducted in different countries. I describe these two types of differences in more detail below.

Cultural differences, societal norms, and interviewing practices

The job interview is among the most popular (if not *the* most popular) selection methods around the world.[40] Almost every selection process, independent of the country, will include some form of interviewing. Furthermore, as mentioned earlier, applicants' reactions to selection methods, including the interview, tend to be quite similar in different countries. For instance, studies conducted in countries as culturally different as the U.S., France, Spain, the Netherlands, Turkey, Singapore, and South Africa found quite consistent positive rections towards interviews.[41] There are, however, some important country-to-country differences in interviewing practices. One main reason is that different countries or regions have different societal values that shape people's attitudes, beliefs, and behaviours in their lives in general, but also in organizational contexts.

In the 1980s, social psychologist Geert Hofstede examined IBM employees around the world. He discovered large cultural differences in the way power was distributed in the organization (or the society), how people reacted to uncertainty, if individuals cared mostly about themselves and their immediate families or a larger community, and whether there was a focus on collaboration vs. competition.[42] Since then, hundreds of studies have explored cultural differences in attitudes or behaviours in a variety of contexts. Alternative cultural models (e.g., the GLOBE cultural dimensions, Schwartz's values, or high- vs. low-context communication cultures) have been developed to describe those differences and add important additional cultural elements. For example, the GLOBE model incoporates the notion of gender equality as well as how much importance is attributed to fairness, altruism, or generosity in a culture.[43] All of these cultural factors can impact the way interviews are designed or conducted because organizations' and interviewers' actions are rooted in cultural norms and values. This has major implications for job applicants, who have to realize that they should expect different interviews in different cultures, but also for organizations. Indeed, a multinational company interested in implementing a specific interview format in offices around the world may experience resistance from managers or interviewers if the format is in conflict with their cultural values or preferences.

For instance, a study examined the format and content of interviews in 20 countries and highlighted interesting patterns and unique practices.[44] For instance, organizations in most countries rely largely on one-on-one interviews, although this seems to be especially prominent in Latin European countries (e.g., France, Italy, Spain, and Greece). Alternatively, panel or group interviews appear to be much more popular in Australia, the U.K., Ireland, and the Netherlands. Organizations in Latin European countries tend to conduct mutliple (i.e., more than three on average) one-on-one interviews, while those in Northern European countries tend to conduct fewer interviews (i.e., close to two on average) but involve a panel of interviewers. Therefore, if Rachel and Kareem are invited to interview for a job in the U.K., they are likely to be interviewed once or twice by a panel of interviewers. However, if the job is in Italy, they should expect to be interviewed individually by three or four people. There are also important differences in the implementation of some other key features of structured interviews that I described in Chapter 2. For instance, I described asking all applicants the same questions for the same job as one of the best practices for interviewing. Yet, the actual percentage of interviewers reporting using fixed interview questions varies from 10% in Italy to 59% in Australia, with countries like Germany (17%) or the U.K. (34%) somewhere in between.[45] It is interesting to note that culturally similar countries do not always adopt the same interviewing practices – for instance, Canadian interviewers seem to be much more avid users of a fixed set of questions than their American neighbours (i.e., 55% vs. 35%).

Cultural differences may also influence the gender of the interviewer, the types of questions asked in the interview, or the chances of getting a job offer after an interview.[46] For instance, some cultures attach more value to equality between men and women than others, which influences the likelihood of women being in an interviewer role. If Rachel and Kareem apply for a job in the U.S., they have about a 50% chance of being interviewed by a woman. However, this is much more likely to happen in countries that strongly value gender egalitarism, like Belgium or Russia, and less likely to be the case in countries were gender is traditionally associated with different roles, like Taiwan or Mexico. Altogether, although research suggests that significant differences in interviewing practices exist between countries, it is important to note that there is no unique country-level approach to interviewing; there are significant differences between organizations within the same country.[47] In other words, if Kareem interviews with two organizations in the U.K., these two experiences may be as different as if he interviewed with companies in two different countries. Yet, it is important to note that research on cultural differences in interviewing practices remains quite limited, and the world is getting more multicultural every day. As such, it is likely that the numbers listed above will have evolved since the studies I relied on were conducted.

International differences in interview-related legislation

In addition to cross-country differences in interviewing practices, countries also differ in employment the legislation that impacts what interviewers can and cannot do. First, countries diverge in their anti-discrimination laws and employment equity programs.[48] For instance, most countries have a number of groups or classes that are protected against discrimination and should receive a fair treatment during the selection process. This implies that interviewers cannot ask questions or evaluate applicants in a way that could penalize those who belong to a protected group. And, in some cases, they may be encouraged to favour applicants from minority groups if two candidates with similar qualifications are assessed. For example, discrimination based on gender, race, or ethnicity is illegal in most countries around the world. Yet, which additional groups are protected may be very different from one country to the next, thus creating unique factors influencing what interviewing practices would be legal or illegal. For instance, in the U.S., race, religion, and sex are protected under Title VII of the Civil Rights Act of 1964. And, additional leglisation has been added to protect age (Age Discrimination in Employment Act) and disability (Rehabilitation Act). The U.K. has similar protections, but also includes protection based on pregancy, sexual orientation, or gender reassignment. In Canada, applicants of Aboriginal ancestry are protected against discrimination, and organizations that are federally regulated must employ a percentage of employees of Aboriginal ancestry that is commensurate with their representation in the Canadian workforce. As such, Canadian interviewers may be encouraged to favour an Aboriginal (or Indigenous) applicant in competition with another candidate with comparable qualifications. Switzerland has four official national languages, and thus it considers one's native language as a protected ground for discrimination. In India, organizations are permitted to use less stringent criteria when assessing applicants from scheduled castes and tribes. In France, Belgium, or Spain, being a member of a professional or labour union is also legally protected. Overall, almost every country has a unique set of anti-discrimination legislation, and interviewers and interview candidates should be aware of those applying to them.

Moreover, some countries have laws and standards that are more strict regarding what topics can be discussed during the interview, what organizations have to do to protect themselves against discrimination claims, or the consequences of legal violations.[49] For instance, in countries like the U.S., organizations that cannot demonstrate that hiring decisions were based on job-related criteria are likely to be sued by rejected or dissatisfied candidates. Other countries, like France or Italy, have more ambiguous or more lenient requirements. In countries were standards and legislation are more ambiguous, interviewers have more freedom in the way they ask questions or assess candidates' performance. As an example, a study showed that candidates like Rachel and Kareem are less likely to be asked questions about their hobbies, personal interests, or families when interviewing in the U.S. compared to places like Taiwan or Russia.[50]

Effective interviewing: A summary

After describing how organizations can design effective interviews in Chapter 2, this third chapter reviewed what applicants and interviewers can do during the interview to make sure that it reaches its full potential. I summarize here what our two candidates, Rachel and Kareem, and our interviewer, Alice, can do to make the interview at Brilliant Electronics optimal.

From the applicants' perspective, effective interviewing necessitates that Rachel and Kareem deal with their anxiety, prepare themselves for the interview, identify what qualities the organization is trying to assess, and manage their expectations. Anxiety can be a major issue for both candidates, whose performance becomes suboptimal and whose chances of getting the job are reduced, and organizations, which can miss out on hiring a potentially competent employee. Rachel and (especially) Kareem can attempt to reduce their anxiety by using emotion-oriented or problem-oriented coping strategies – for instance, by discussing their anxiety with friends before the interview or by getting ready for potential questions that could be asked during the interview. Our two candidates can also engage in activities (e.g., gathering information about the hiring organization, reading books, participating in training sessions) to be as ready as they can be when they enter the interview room.

Ideally, Rachel and Kareem should study Brilliant Electronics and the engineer job description, anticipate possible interview questions, think about past experiences or accomplishments that would be pertinent to such questions, and prepare a set of narratives to use when answering questions. This strategy would be even more effective if our two candidates possess high levels of ATIC – that is, if they are capable of identifying what qualities (e.g., skills, abilities, competencies, etc.) Brilliant Electronics is looking for in potential engineers. More specific suggestions are provided in the "Toolbox" at the end of this chapter. Finally, Rachel and Kareem should strive to set realistic pre-interview expectations, because expectations that are too high or too low will serve as anchors and may bias their reactions to the interview. Once again, this can be achieved mostly by gathering more information about the job and the organization. Alice also has an important role to play and can help candidates by providing information about the forthcoming interviewing process.

From the interviewer's perspective, effective interviewing will require Alice to understand applicants' reactions and ensure a fair selection process. Although interviews are usually perceived positively by applicants, compared to other selection methods, Alice needs to highlight that all applicants are interviewed the same way and treated respectfully. She also needs to ensure that Kareem, Rachel, and the other candidates understand why they are asked questions about job-related past experiences or hypothetical scenarios, and she should provide them with guidance on how to respond. Importantly, Alice should be very careful regarding how hiring decisions are communicated to applicants. She should inform all candidates of the outcome, and she should be particularly vigilant when dealing with rejected candidates, who can easily share their frustrations with their networks and indirectly hurt the organization's reputation. Rejection decisions should be justifed, but they should focus on the process rather than the potential weaknesses of unsuccessful applicants.

Finally, what is considered effective interviewing may differ from one country to the next. Although globalization tends to facilitate the standardization of processes and the recommendations provided above (and in Chapter 2) should ideally be applied all around the world, it is important to take into account cultural and legal differences. Who is (or how many people are) conducting the interview, what kind of questions are perceived as being acceptable, and what characteristics are used to assess candidates may vary if Rachel and Kareem interview for an engineering position in Europe, North America, or Asia (and vary between and within countries in those regions, as well).

Chapter 3 – Toolbox

Prepare for Interviews: Improve your ATIC and become a STAR	
Step 1	This is where you can use and improve your ability to identify criteria (i.e., ATIC). Try to identify what skills, abilities, values, experiences, etc. the hiring organization will likely be assessing in the interview: • Carefully read the <u>job advertisement</u> (e.g., role description and qualifications, list of required skills or experience) • Consult the <u>company website</u> (and/or career website if they have one) to identify culture, values, etc. • If possible, reach out to <u>connections</u> you might have within the organization (e.g., family, friends, alumni) for their insights • Consult <u>online job descriptions</u>, which can provide valuable information about a variety of jobs, such as O*NET in the U.S. (https://www.onetonline.org), NOC in Canada (https://noc.esdc.gc.ca), or SOC in the UK (https://www.ons.gov.uk/methodology/classificationsandstandards).

continued . . .

(Continued)

Step 2	List the possible job requirements (from Step 1) and consider what kinds of questions interviewers might ask for each of them. Check some example questions in the Chapter 2 "Toolbox" as a starting point.
Step 3	Think about your own experiences (work, school, volunteering, etc.). Try to find at least one relevant experience for each job requirement or potential question from Step 2 – that is, find experiences where you demonstrate the requirement (e.g., applied the skills or successfully accomplished something). It is OK to have multiple experiences for each question or to use the same experience for a few questions.
Step 4	For each potential question, use the STAR technique to describe the relevant past experience or emphasize your qualifications. Describe your experience using the following four components: 1. <u>Situation</u> – What was the context, when did it happen, what problem did you face? 2. <u>Task</u> – What was your role, position, or responsibilities (e.g., leadership role vs. team member)? 3. <u>Action</u> – How did you react, what actions did you take, what decisions did you make? 4. <u>Result</u> – What was the result or outcome for you, your team, or your organization? *Note that interviewers are also encouraged to use the content presented here (e.g., STAR approach) either to provide some guidelines for applicants at the start of their interview or when probing or following-up on applicants' responses.*
Step 5	Practice responding to interview questions using the STAR format: • Just by yourself or in front of your mirror • Record yourself and then watch your performance • Ask a friend to help you do practice interviews and provide feedback

Notes

1 Derous, E., and K. De Witte, *Looking at selection from a social process perspective: Towards a social process model on personnel selection.* European Journal of Work and Organizational Psychology, 2001. **10**: p. 319–342.

2 McCarthy, J.M., and R. Goffin, *Measuring job interview anxiety: Beyond weak knees and sweat palms.* Personnel Psychology, 2004. **51**(3): p. 607–637; Constantin, K.L., D.M. Powell, and J.M. McCarthy, *Expanding conceptual understanding of interview anxiety and performance: Integrating cognitive, behavioral, and physiological features.* International Journal of Selection and Assessment, 2021. **29**(2): p. 234–252.

3 Feiler, A.R., and D.M. Powell, *Behavioral expression of job interview anxiety.* Journal of Business and Psychology, 2015. **31**(1): p. 155–171.

4 Feiler, A.R., and D.M. Powell, *Behavioral expression of job interview anxiety.* Journal of Business and Psychology, 2015. **31**(1): p. 155–171.

5 McCarthy, J.M., and R. Goffin, *Measuring job interview anxiety: Beyond weak knees and sweaty palms.* Personnel Psychology, 2004. **51**(3): p. 607–637; Powell, D.M., D.J. Stanley, and K.N. Brown, *Meta-analysis of the relation between interview anxiety and interview performance.* Canadian Journal of Behavioural Science/Revue canadienne des sciences du comportement, 2018. **50**(4): p. 195.

6 Schneider, L., D.M. Powell, and S. Bonaccio, *Does interview anxiety predict job performance and does it influence the predictive validity of interviews?* International Journal of Selection and Assessment, 2019. **27**(4): p. 328–336.

7 Feeney, J.R., J.M. McCarthy, and R. Goffin, *Applicant anxiety: Examining the sex-linked anxiety coping theory in job interview contexts.* International Journal of Selection and Assessment, 2015. **23**(3): p. 295–305.

8 Feeney, J.R., J.M. McCarthy, and R. Goffin, *Applicant anxiety: Examining the sex-linked anxiety coping theory in job interview contexts.* International Journal of Selection and Assessment, 2015. **23**(3): p. 295–305.

9 Hecht, T.D., and J.M. McCarthy, *Coping with employee, family, and student roles: Evidence of dispositional conflict and facilitation tendencies.* Journal of Applied Psychology, 2010. **95**(4): p. 631–647.

10 Roulin, N., and A. Bangerter, *Les livres de conseils: Un moyen de réduire l'incertitude des candidats liée à l'entretien de sélection [Advice books: A way to reduce applicants' uncertainty due to the selection interview].* Psychologie du Travail et des Organisations, 2012(17): p. 426–444.

11 Palmer, D.K., M.A. Campion, and P.C. Green, *Interviewing training for both applicant and interviewer,* in *The employment interview handbook,* R.W. Eder and M.M. Harris, Editors. 1999, Sage: Thousand Oaks, CA. p. 337–351.

12 Palmer, D.K., M.A. Campion, and P.C. Green, *Interviewing training for both applicant and interviewer,* in *The employment interview handbook,* R.W. Eder and M.M. Harris, Editors. 1999, Sage: Thousand Oaks, CA. p. 337–351.

13 Knudstrup, M., S.L. Segrest, and A.E. Hurley, *The use of mental imagery in the simulated employment interview situation.* Journal of Managerial Psychology, 2003. **18**(6): p. 573–591.

14 Maurer, T.J., et al., *Interviewee coaching, preparation strategies, and response strategies in relation to performance in situational employment interviews: An extension of Maurer, Solamon, and Troxtel (1998).* Journal of Applied Psychology, 2001. **86**(4): p. 709–717.

15 Stewart, G.L., et al., *Exploring the handshake in employment interviews.* Journal of Applied Psychology, 2008. **93**: p. 1139–1146.

16 Maurer, T.J., J.M. Solamon, and M. Lippstreu, *How does coaching interviewees affect the validity of a structured interview?* Journal of Organizational Behavior, 2008. **29**(3): p. 355–371.

17 Kleinmann, M., et al., *A different look at why selection procedures work: The role of candidates' ability to identify criteria.* Organizational Psychology Review, 2011. **1**: p. 128–146.

18 Melchers, K.G., et al., *"I know what you want to know": The impact of interviewees' ability to identify criteria on interview performance and construct-related validity.* Human Performance, 2009. **22**(4): p. 355–374.

19 Kleinmann, M., et al., *A different look at why selection procedures work: The role of candidates' ability to identify criteria.* Organizational Psychology Review, 2011. **1**: p. 128–146.

20 Buehl, A.-K., et al., *Tell Me Sweet Little Lies: How Does Faking in Interviews Affect Interview Scores and Interview Validity?* Journal of Business and Psychology, 2019. **34**: p. 107–124.

21 Schmidt, F.L., and J.E. Hunter, *General mental ability in the world of work: Occupational attainment and job performance.* Journal of Personality and Social Psychology, 2004. **86**: p. 162–173.

22 Klehe, U.-C., et al., *Transparency in structured interviews: Consequences for construct and criterion-related validity.* Human Performance, 2008. **21**(2): p. 107–137.

23 Schreurs, B., et al., *Applicant selection expectations: Validating a multidimensional measure in the military.* International Journal of Selection and Assessment, 2008. **16**(2): p. 170–176.

24 Schreurs, B., et al., *The relation between selection expectations, perceptions, and organizational attraction: A test of competing models.* International Journal of Selection and Assessment, 2010. **18**(4): p. 447–452.

25 Bell, B.S., D. Wiechmann, and A.M. Ryan, *Consequences of organizational justice expectations in a selection system.* Journal of Applied Psychology, 2006. **91**(2): p. 455–466.

26 Schreurs, B., et al., *The relation between selection expectations, perceptions, and organizational attraction: A test of competing models.* International Journal of Selection and Assessment, 2010. **18**(4): p. 447–452.

27 Bell, B.S., A.M. Ryan, and D. Wiechmann, *Justice expectations and applicant perceptions.* International Journal of Selection and Assessment, 2004. **12**(1–2): p. 24–38.

28 McCarthy, J.M., et al., *Applicant perspectives during selection: A review addressing "so what?", "what's new?", and "where to next?".* Journal of Management, 2017. **43**(6): p. 1693–1725.

29 Anderson, N., J.F. Salgado, and U.R. Hülsheger, *Applicant reactions in selection: Comprehensive meta-analysis into reaction generalization versus situational specificity.* International Journal of Selection and Assessment, 2010. **18**(3): p. 291–304.

30 Van Hoye, G., and F. Lievens, *Social influences on organizational attractiveness: Investigating if and when word of mouth matters.* Journal of Applied Social Psychology, 2007. **37**(9): p. 2024–2047.

31   McCarthy, J.M., et al., *Applicant perspectives during selection: A review addressing "so what?", "what's new?", and "where to next?"*. Journal of Management, 2017. **43**(6): p. 1693–1725.

32   Anderson, N., J.F. Salgado, and U.R. Hülsheger, *Applicant reactions in selection: Comprehensive meta-analysis into reaction generalization versus situational specificity.* International Journal of Selection and Assessment, 2010. **18**(3): p. 291–304.

33   Gilliland, S.W., *The perceived fairness of selection systems: An organizational justice perspective.* Academy of Management Review, 1993. **18**: p. 694–734.

34   Levashina, J., et al., *The structured employment interview: Narrative and quantitative review of the research literature.* Personnel Psychology, 2014. **67**(1): p. 241–293.

35   Petruzziello, G., et al., *The role of feedback on interview self-efficacy and outcome expectations.* International Journal of Selection and Assessment, 2021. DOI: 10.1111/ijsa.12334.

36   Waung, M., and T.S. Brice, *The effect of acceptance/rejection status, status notification, and organizational obligation fulfillment on applicant intentions.* Journal of Applied Social Psychology, 2007. **37**(9): p. 2048–2071.

37   Truxillo, D.M., et al., *Effects of explanations on applicant reactions: A meta-analytic review.* International Journal of Selection and Assessment, 2009. **17**(4): p. 346–361.

38   Schinkel, S., et al., *Applicant reactions to rejection: Feedback, fairness, and attributional style effects.* Journal of Personnel Psychology, 2011. **10**(4): p. 146–156.

39   Schinkel, S., D. Van Dierendonck, and N. Anderson, *The impact of selection encounters on applicants: An experimental study into feedback effects after a negative selection decision.* International Journal of Selection and Assessment, 2004. **12**(1–2): p. 197–205.

40   Steiner, D.D., *Personnel selection across the globe*, in *The Oxford Handbook of Personnel Assessment and Selection*, N. Schmitt, Editor. 2012, Oxford University Press: New York. p. 740–767.

41   Anderson, N., J.F. Salgado, and U.R. Hülsheger, *Applicant reactions in selection: Comprehensive meta-analysis into reaction generalization versus situational specificity.* International Journal of Selection and Assessment, 2010. **18**(3): p. 291–304; Anderson, N., and C. Witvliet, *Fairness reactions to personnel selection methods: An international comparison between the Netherlands, the United States, France, Spain, Portugal, and Singapore.* International Journal of Selection and Assessment, 2008. **16**(1): p. 1–13.

42   Hofstede, G., *Culture's consequences: Comparing values, behaviors, institutions, and organizations across nations.* 2001, Thousand Oaks, CA: Sage Publications.

43   House, R., et al., *Understanding cultures and implicit leadership theories across the globe: An introduction to project GLOBE.* Journal of World Business, 2002. **37**(1): p. 3–10.

44   Ryan, A.M., et al., *An international look at selection practices: Nation and culture as explanations for variability in practice.* Personnel Psychology, 1999. **52**: p. 359–391.

45   Ryan, A.M., et al., *An international look at selection practices: Nation and culture as explanations for variability in practice.* Personnel Psychology, 1999. **52**: p. 359–391.

46 Posthuma, R.A., et al., *Comparing employment interviews in Latin America with other countries*. Journal of Business Research, 2014. **67**(5): p. 943–951.

47 Ryan, A.M., et al., *An international look at selection practices: Nation and culture as explanations for variability in practice*. Personnel Psychology, 1999. **52**: p. 359–391.

48 Myors, B., et al., *International Perspectives on the Legal Environment for Selection*. Industrial and Organizational Psychology, 2008. **1**(2): p. 206–246.

49 Myors, B., et al., *International Perspectives on the Legal Environment for Selection*. Industrial and Organizational Psychology, 2008. **1**(2): p. 206–246.

50 Posthuma, R.A., et al., *Comparing employment interviews in Latin America with other countries*. Journal of Business Research, 2014. **67**(5): p. 943–951.

Playing your role

How applicants
and interviewers
can influence
interview
outcomes

Applicants' and interviewers' objectives in job interviews

Box 4.1

Rachel and Kareem are both interviewing today with Louis, the HR manager of Power Engine. Although Rachel believes that her first interview with Future Technology was quite successful, she has not heard back from them. And she thinks that her second interview at Brilliant Electronics is unlikely to lead to a positive outcome. Kareem's situation is even worse because he perceives his first two interviews as major failures. Overall,

continued . . .

DOI: 10.4324/9781003171089-4

cont.

both of our candidates are particularly motivated to perform well in the third interview and land an engineering job at Power Engine. Louis's position is not ideal either. His company just lost a number of talented engineers to a competitor, hence the need to recruit for several positions in the next few weeks. Moreover, Louis's last hire, Eve, ended up being a major failure. Eve largely exaggerated her qualifications during her interview with Louis to get hired. She later made a number of critical mistakes with her first important client, and the company had to fire her after only two weeks on the job.

Taken together, the specific challenges faced by our two candidates and our interviewer create a rather complex situation. On the applicants' side, Rachel and Kareem have experienced rather unsuccessful interviews so far and are starting to feel the pressure to find a job. If they are unemployed, paying the bills may become difficult, and they may need to rapidly secure employment. They may also have realized that they are competing with other job seekers for a relatively small number of positions, and thus they need to "up their game" to increase their chances of success. As such, both really want to impress Louis during the interview. To achieve this objective, Rachel and Kareem may decide to use a variety of tactics (that psychology researchers often call *impression management* tactics) to influence Louis's evaluation during the interview.

On the organization's side, Louis is also under pressure to find and secure qualified candidates to compensate for the recent departures. Therefore, he may also be interested in engaging in impression management to convince candidates like Rachel and Kareem that Power Engine is a great place to work, and they should accept a subsequent job offer. At the same time, Louis also wants to ensure that the chosen candidates are actually the best fit for the job (and indirectly erase

continued . . .

> **cont.**
>
> the mistake he made with Eve). He might thus be skeptical towards applicants and will be particularly motivated to detect exaggerated or deceitful statements that Rachel, Kareem, or other candidates may use.

This type of situation is not exceptional. Indeed, the selection process, and job interviews in particular, often involves applicants and interviewers whose interests are not perfectly aligned.[1] Therefore, in this fourth chapter, I highlight tactics or strategies that job applicants and interviewers can use to influence evaluations made by the other party. In the first part of the chapter, I describe the growing body of psychology research on impression management tactics that applicants can use. I show that candidates can rely on such tactics to highlight their qualities, praise the interviewer or organization, and protect their image of a good applicant. Although influence tactics are mostly used to highlight applicants' true qualifications, they can also become deceptive (also known as *applicant faking*) – for instance, when exaggerating, inventing, or hiding information to create a better impression. I also describe whether the use of influence tactics is determined by applicants' individual characteristics or the situation they are facing, the impact of such tactics on interview outcomes, and interviewers' attempts to detect when applicants are using them. In parallel, this chapter reviews impression management tactics that interviewers can use – for instance, presenting an image of competence or influencing applicants' acceptance of a potential job offer.

Applicants' influence tactics

This is how we play our part: Tactics that applicants can use

If Rachel and Kareem want to impress Louis during their interview, what tactics or strategies can they use? There are actually three broad forms of influence tactics that job applicants can use during an interview: *self-focused*, *other-focused*, and *defensive* tactics.[2] When they use *self-focused* tactics, candidates generally engage in self-promotion. That is, they make sure that their answers present their knowledge, skills, abilities, or accomplishments in a positive light. For instance, imagine that Louis asks Rachel to describe a past situation when she led a team, and Rachel decides to describe her role as vice-president of an association of engineering students on campus. She can present this experience in a modest way by downplaying her leadership role and highlighting team achievements. Alternatively, she can engage in self-promotion by stressing how important her vice-president role was in the association, describing major projects she was responsible for, emphasizing how her leadership style helped motivate teams of several individuals, and underlining her key contributions to the success of projects. Using self-promotion may look like the logical way to answer any interview question, and it is indeed the most popular type of influence tactic. For instance, research suggests that candidates use self-promotion tactics more than 30 times per interview on average.[3] Yet, not all job applicants use such an approach to a large extent. Some people prefer to remain modest or present their achievements as the result of team efforts.

The second type of tactic that candidates can engage in is *other-focused*, such as ingratiation. Contrary to self-promotion, which is focused on the applicants themselves, ingratiation is focused on the interviewer or the hiring organization.[4] When ingratiation is focused on the interviewer, the objective is to create a psychological connection between the interviewer and the candidate. Let's imagine that Kareem enters Louis's office for his interview and immediately notices a shelf populated with a number of small robots. Kareem can logically infer from this collection that Louis likes robots. You may remember from Chapter 2 that Kareem participated in robot competitions when he was a student. He may thus use ingratiation to highlight this common interest. For example, he might choose to directly mention his passion for robots during the initial rapport-building phase of the interview, in the hope that Louis will initiate some small talk around that topic, which might create a positive initial impression. Or, Kareem could strategically use his robot competition experience when answering a question later on in the interview. Furthermore, Kareem could try to praise the interviewer (e.g., by stressing his admiration of Louis's impressive robot collection) or con-form with his opinion (e.g., by agreeing with Louis's statements that robots are the future of engineering). Other-focused tactics may help Kareem create an impression of similarity with Louis. And, psychology research has demonstrated that interviewers are more favourable towards candidates that they perceive are similar to them.[5] Kareem's ingratiation tactics can thus possibly make Louis's evaluation of his responses (or his overall interview performance) more positive.

Alternatively, ingratiation tactics can also be oriented towards the organization to accentuate interviewers' view of the perceived fit between the applicant's values, beliefs, and motives and those of the organization.[6] The objective is to increase the perception of person-organization (or P-O) fit described in Chapter 1.[7] Let's imagine that Power Engine is a "green" organization. It specializes in developing car engines that rely on sustainable sources of energy (e.g., for electric or hybrid vehicles), values nature conservation, and encourages all employees to save energy and recycle. Rachel happens to share those values. She is very involved in recycling at home, and she regularly volunteers to clean local parks and plant trees during her free time. She may thus benefit from highlighting how her values fit with Power Engine's during the interview. For instance, when answering a question about initiative or teamwork, she could use her volunteering experience and particularly highlight its "green" aspects. In addition to demonstrating that she possesses valuable skills, Rachel would be using ingratiation to convince Louis that she is a perfect fit with Power Engine in terms of core values.

Finally, applicants can use *defensive* tactics to protect or repair their image and ensure that they are perceived by the interviewer as good and competent candidates. Contrary to assertive or proactive tactics like self-promotion and ingratiation, defensive tactics are more reactive. They are used by candidates only when necessary, notably when an interviewer raises some concerns regarding the individual's competence or integrity.[8] In such cases, applicants have to react by providing justifications, excuses, or apologies. For instance, let's imagine that Kareem was required to provide a transcript of his university grades as part of his application package. Louis notices that Kareem grade for his Engineering Design class is rather low and asks him what happened. Kareem's image is threatened by this question, and he is forced to justify the low grade. For instance, he may highlight that the professor's grading system was particularly demanding, and his grade was simply equivalent to the class average. By doing so, Kareem protects his image as a good candidate in Louis's eyes. The same approach can be used to justify why candidates left previous jobs (e.g., because there were no growth opportunities) or why they were unemployed for a period of time (e.g., to reorient their career). Sometimes a negative aspect of one's employment history or past behaviours cannot be easily justified. In such cases, applicants cannot completely eliminate the threat, but they may attempt to minimize it by accepting responsibility, apologizing, and highlighting how they learnt from their mistakes. For instance, Louis may notice that Rachel was fired from a part-time job when she was a teenager. To defend her image, Rachel may admit that she made a mistake (e.g., she was late several times) and explain that she was young and less dependable at that time. She could follow-up by describing the steps she took to change and highlighting her progress and subsequent successes in more recent jobs.

In addition to the three types of verbal impression management tactics described above, job applicants can also engage in a variety of non-verbal tactics. People are generally able to strategically control or adapt the way they behave for self-presentation purposes, and this is especially true in job interviews.[9] For instance, Kareem could make sure to smile regularly when interacting with Louis, make frequent eye contact with him, and nod to emphasize his agreement with (or understanding of) what Louis is saying. Using such non-verbal tactics in conjunction with verbal tactics may also make the candidate's argument more persuasive. If Rachel makes eye contact with Louis while describing her leadership experience and concludes her response with a confident smile, her performance may be perceived as even more convincing.

The dark side of the force: Deceptive tactics and faking

The types of tactics described in the previous section correspond to behaviours that are usually expected from applicants. Indeed, interviewers expect candidates to promote their qualifications, ingratiate themselves, and defend their image if needed.[10] Yet, such behaviours can be considered acceptable only if they are aligned with the true qualities (and potential weaknesses) of the candidates. Unfortunately, the last decade of industrial psychology research has highlighted that job applicants are not always completely authentic in their responses. More precisely, instead of (or in addition to) honest impression management tactics, applicants may also engage in deceptive tactics, also known as *applicant faking*.[11] The distinction between honest and deceptive influence tactics is very important, because the interviewer wants to know if applicants truly possesses job-related qualifications and values matching those of the organization, or if they are simply pretending to possess them.[12] While deceptive tactics are less prevalent than honest ones, they are still used by many job candidates. For instance, in one study 81% of applicants admitted telling at least one lie in their last interview, with an average of 2.19 lies per interview.[13]

Box 4.2

Imagine that Louis wants to assess Kareem's initiative and asks him to describe a situation where he took the initiative to create something that was valuable for his organization. Kareem provides the following response:

When I was working at Advanced Telecom last summer, my manager got me involved in a project with an important client. As part of the project, he gave me the opportunity to propose a new design for a piece of telecommunication equipment. I spent dozens of hours after work thinking about this design, looking at what our competitors' products looked like, and coming up with a new design, which included a number of really original features. My manager loved the idea and allowed me to present it to the client. The client was very enthusiastic, and the whole project was adapted to work on that design. Since then, similar designs have been used by Advanced Telecom in very lucrative projects with over 20 other clients.

Based on the previous section, one could argue that Kareem provided a convincing answer, largely because he engaged in self-promotion to highlight a successful experience. If Kareem's response is 100% genuine (i.e., if he used honest impression

continued . . .

---

cont.

management to present actual behaviours and factual events in a positive light), then Louis can easily and reliably infer that Kareem is able to take initiative. But what if Kareem's answer is not entirely honest? Maybe he slightly embellished his accomplishment – for instance, taking all of the credit for something that was actually a team effort or exaggerating the number of subsequent projects that used his design. Or maybe he even made up that experience, or he stole it from someone else – for instance, the colleague who actually came up with the new design. If that is the case, Louis's evaluation of Kareem's initiative skills could be overrated because it is based on (partly) falsified information.

It is also important to highlight that deceptive impression management (or faking) by applicants can take different forms. Indeed, industrial psychology researchers have found that the three types of influence tactics described in the previous section exist both in honest and deceptive forms.[14] The example about initiative presented above illustrates a potentially deceptive form of self-promotion, which researchers have called *image creation*. Image creation involves embellishing, exaggerating, inventing, or borrowing knowledge, skills, abilities, or experiences in order to appear more qualified for the job. Moreover, applicants can use *deceptive ingratiation* – that is, pretend to conform with the values and opinions of the interviewer or the organization while actually disagreeing with or insincerely praising them. For instance, Rachel may see Louis's robot collection and pretend to be fascinated by robots, although she really has no interest in them. Kareem may learn that Power Engine values green behaviours and pretend to share those values, even though he does not particularly care about the environment. In both situations, the candidates use deceptive tactics in order to create a fictitious perception of similarity or P-O fit in the interviewer's mind.

Finally, candidates can use deceptive defensive tactics, labelled *image protection*. Such tactics may involve omitting or masking negative facts that may harm the applicant's image. For instance, instead of assuming responsibility for a mistake in an earlier job that led to her being fired, Rachel may decide to hide the true reason for this negative outcome (e.g., claim that her boss had a personal grudge against her) or pretended that she was not fired but chose to quit on her own. Although not all job applicants engage in deceptive impression management (or engage in those tactics to the same extent), research suggests that an important proportion do. For instance, a review of the literature on faking showed that, across seven studies, between 44% and 99% of applicants engaged at least to some extent in some form of embellishment or exaggeration.[15]

Born to influence or pressured to influence? What makes applicants use influence tactics

Since the beginning of psychology research, academics have examined whether people's abilities, attitudes, or behaviours are innate or acquired – that is, whether people are born with them, or they are learned over time. Often, the response to that fundamental question is "both." We know, for instance, that an individual's personality is influenced by characteristics inherited at birth, but it is also shaped by education or environment while growing up. Nowadays, many psychology studies investigate a slightly different version of this question and focus on whether behaviours are caused by stable individual characteristics like personality, intelligence, and core values, or whether they are dependent on the situation or the environment one is facing. In the case of influence tactics in job interviews, researchers have examined whether an applicant uses such tactics because of their unique and stable personality or values (i.e., born to influence) or because of the way the interview is conducted or the broader context the applicant is in (i.e., pressured to influence). Again, the response seems to be "both." More precisely, researchers tend to agree that an applicant's use of influence tactics (or faking) depends on three factors: their motivation or willingness to use influence tactics, their capacity to (effectively) engage in the tactics, and the opportunities offered to them to engage in such behaviours.[16] The willingness and capacity parts are mostly a function of an applicant's individual characteristics, but they also involve cultural factors, whereas the opportunity to influence mostly depends on the context and format of the interview.

Let's start with the individual characteristics. What are the attributes of job applicants who are more likely to use influence tactics – and especially deceptive tactics – in job interviews? Interestingly, earlier research did not find very robust individual characteristics associated with the use of impression management tactics in general.[17] However, more recent work has highlighted a number of personality traits and other stable characteristics that are clearly associated with applicants' use of specific honest or deceptive tactics.[18] In Box 4.3 below, I describe the profiles of applicants who are likely to be *honest* or to *fake* during interviews.

Box 4.3

The Honest Applicants: Interestingly, there are relatively few individual characteristics associated with applicants who are able to honestly describe their qualifications and accomplishments in interviews. They tend to be more extraverted – that is, comfortable in social situations, enjoy gatherings, and quite self-confident. They tend to be also slightly higher on the trait of *conscientiousness*, meaning that they are somewhat more disciplined, careful, or organized. There is also evidence that applicants who are older, more experienced, or have received more interview training tend to use more honest tactics to impress interviewers.

The Fakers: In contrast, applicants who fake tend to demonstrate low levels of the core personality trait of *conscientiousness*, meaning that they are not particularly disciplined, careful, or organized. They also demonstrate low levels of *honesty* but high levels of *psychopathy*, *Machiavellianism*, and *Narcissism*, also known as the *dark triad* of personality. Machiavellianism comes from the Italian politician and writer Niccolò Machiavelli, who was famous for describing how effective deceit and manipulation are in politics. Being Machiavellian, fakers will not

continued . . .

---

cont.

hesitate to manipulate others to achieve personal goals and have no problem with engaging in deceptive influence tactics to increase their chances of succeeding at the interview. Narcissism comes from Narcissus, a young character in the Greek mythology, who fell in love with his own reflection. Being Narcissistic, fakers tend to be selfish, have grandiose views of themselves, and seek others' approval, and they will use deceptive tactics to obtain higher evaluations from an interviewer. They also possess more *Competitive Worldviews*, meaning that they perceive the world as a jungle where everyone must fight others to obtain scarce resources. Fakers thus see an interview as another competitive situation, where it is necessary to do whatever it takes to obtain the job before another applicant takes it away from them. They also view the act of faking as something that is under their control and "normal" (i.e., they believe faking is the norm and other candidates fake too). There is also some evidence that younger applicants tend to fake more, likely in order to compensate for a lack of relevant work experience.

This description of the characteristics of honest and deceptive applicants is particularly interesting for interviewers and organizations. Indeed, psychology research has found that the individual characteristics that comprise fakers' profiles are not only associated with increased deception in interviews, but also with lower job performance and the likelihood of engaging in other counterproductive or undesirable workplace behaviours, such as absenteeism or theft.[19] In contrast, the rare traits associated with honest applicants (e.g., extraversion and conscientiousness) tend to be positively associated with work performance.[20] To put it simply: fakers are *not* the kinds of employee that organizations should be hiring, but honest applicants are!

Applicants' use of influence tactics can also be impacted by cultural norms and values. Although most of the initial research has been conducted in North America or Western Europe, recent studies have highlighted interesting international or cross-cultural differences in applicants' attitudes towards influence tactics or faking as well as their use of such tactics in interviews.[21] For instance, applicants tend to have *more positive* attitudes towards faking in countries that are characterized by high *power distance* (i.e., that accept power to be concentrated at higher levels of organizations or the government) and *collectivism* (i.e., that value the welfare of one's family or organization over the individual), like in China, India, Morocco, or Russia. However, applicants tend to have *more negative* attitudes towards faking in countries that are characterized by high *uncertainty avoidance* (i.e., that rely on strong social norms, rituals, and bureaucracy to limit uncertainty) and *gender egalitarianism* (i.e., that see men and women as having equivalent roles to play in their homes, businesses, or communities), like in Scandinavian or Germanic countries. This implies that candidates are more or less likely to perceive deceptive tactics in interviews as an acceptable practice, and subsquently they fake more or less depending on the culture they are from. In a series of studies in five countries comparing applicant deceptive tactics in interviews, Chinese and American applicants reported using more deception than Swiss or Icelandic ones, while applicants from the United Arab Emirates were in-between.[22] For example, 45% of U.S. and 39% of Chinese candidates admitted having exaggerated their work experience to make themselves look more impressive, whereas only 15% of Emiratis and 8% of Icelandic candidates (and no Swiss) used such a tactic. There are also differences between individuals within each country. For instance, a study comparing the intentions to fake of individuals living in the 50 largest Metropolitan Statistical Areas in the U.S. found interesting regional differences, with the highest intentions around New York and the lowest around Seattle.[23] Overall, interviewers should thus expect the baseline use of tactics to be different between countries or even between regions.

Beyond individual and cultural characteristics, there can also be situational elements that encourage applicants to use influence tactics, especially deceptive ones. For instance, research suggests that applicants are more willing to fake if they are facing a more competitive hiring process or if the culture or climate of the hiring organization is more competitive.[24] In other words, Rachel and Kareem might be more motivated to embellish or exaggerate their qualifications if they realize that they are competing against a lot of (qualified) candidates for the job at Power Engine. Or they might more likely to engage in deceptive behaviours if they visit Power Engine's website and realize that the company emphasizes a "winning at all costs" type of mentality (in contrast to a much more collaborative culture at Brilliant Electronics, for example).

The interview format is a last factor that may impact applicants' use of influence tactics. So, is there a way for Louis to conduct the interview to facilitate honest tactics and discourage deceptive ones? Louis can create different opportunities for applicants to use different types of influence tactics depending on the questions he chooses to ask.[25] If Louis asks Kareem a past-behavioural question (e.g., "Tell me about a time when ..."), Kareem has to describe a past experience, which creates an occasion for him to highlight his accomplishments and thus engage in self-promotion. In contrast, if Louis asks Rachel a situational question (e.g., "Imagine that ..."), Rachel has an opportunity to identify what the organization would perceive as being an ideal behaviour and thus engage in ingratiation (especially if she has strong ATIC, as discussed in Chapter 3). Moreover, although there is no silver bullet that completely prevents the use of deceptive impression management, there are ways to conduct the interview to limit opportunities for applicants to engage in such tactics.[26] For instance, if Louis relies on the type of interview presented in Chapter 2 (e.g., makes the process more standardized, uses behavioural questions instead of *traditional* questions, invites colleagues to form a panel of interviewers, etc.), the opportunities for applicants to engage in deceptive influence tactics are likely to be reduced (albeit not completely eliminated). However, probing or follow-up questions may be perceived by applicants as an invitation to engage in more impression management or faking.[27]

Does it matter? Influence tactics and interview outcomes

Because most candidates are likely to engage in influence tactics during their interviews, a key practical question for both applicants and interviewers is whether or not using such tactics is likely to impact the outcome of the interview. The short answer is "yes." Overall, using influence tactics is likely to benefit the applicant, as it leads to more positive evaluations by the interviewer.[28] However, the more comprehensive answer is that it depends on the type of tactic used and how it is used. Self-promotion tactics have the largest impact on interviewers' ratings. As such, Kareem and Rachel may benefit from emphasizing their qualities, experiences, and accomplishments in their answers in order to receive a more positive evaluation from Louis. Ingratiation, defensive tactics, and non-verbal tactics will also lead to more positive ratings, although their effect is likely to be weaker. Honest self-promotion and ingratiation tactics seem to be particularly effective in impressing interviewers.[29] Why? Because interviewers perceive applicants who use more honest self-promotion as more competent and those who use more honest ingratiation as warmer, friendlier, and more trustworthy.[30] However, there is also evidence that, beyond a certain point, using extensive amounts of self-promotion can backfire.[31] This means that applicants like Rachel and Kareem should engage in honest influence tactics, but do so with moderation. Otherwise, they might be perceived as arrogant and bragging.

What about deceptive tactics? Research in that area is relatively limited, and results presented by different researchers are not always aligned. One of the first studies compared the probability of a job applicant receiving a positive outcome (i.e., getting a job offer or being invited for a second interview) depending on the type of deceptive tactic used.[32] Deceptive self-promotion (i.e., image creation) tactics were associated with positive outcomes, while deceptive defensive tactics were associated with negative outcomes. More precisely, applicants who used only deceptive defensive tactics – that is, hid negative information or experiences to protect their image – had lower chances of getting a positive evaluation; those who decided to not use any deceptive tactics had moderate chances of getting a positive evaluation; and those who extensively engaged in image creation – that is, exaggerated or invented qualities or accomplishments to appear more qualified – had higher chances getting a positive evaluation. However, this initial study was based on a small group of U.S. students as applicants. A more recent estimation, based on the combined findings of 27 studies, found that interview faking was largely unrelated to interview performance.[33] In other words, applicants who faked did not experience any benefits (nor any drawbacks) from doing so!

Let's summarize what we know about deceptive tactics to emphasize the importance of the evidence described above:

(1) Although not all job applicants engage in deceptive tactics, a non-
negligible proportion of them do use such tactics in interviews.
(2) Candidates who are more likely to fake tend to have a number of
negative characteristics. They lack conscientiousness, which is the
personality trait most strongly associated with job performance.
They also tend to be dishonest, Machiavellian, and Narcissistic – a
personality profile associated with counterproductive behaviours
at work.
(3) Candidates usually engage in deceptive tactics because they are
less experienced, to compensate for a lack of job-related skills or
abilities, or because they perceive the hiring situation to be more
competitive. Therefore, they are likely to be less qualified for the
position than applicants using only honest influence tactics.
(4) When candidates do fake in the interview, it tends to not be
rewarded by the interviewer. Nevertheless, there are exceptions.
In such cases, organizations are potentially facing a very important problem, because less qualified individuals may use deceptive
influence tactics to get hired over more qualified ones who do not
use such tactics.

There is also a growing consensus among interview researchers that
such behaviours may limit interviewers' ability to reliably assess applicants' qualities and accurately predict their capacity to perform on the
job.[34] In other words, applicants' deceptive tactics may be a threat to
the reliability and validity of the interview. Unfortunately, psychology
research has just started to accumulate empirical evidence about the
risks associated with applicant faking tactics, and effective potential
solutions for eliminating this threat are still limited.

Catch me if you can: Interviewers' attempts to detect influence tactics

So what can organizations do to solve (or at least lessen) the faking problem? In theory, the easier solution would be to rely on

interviewers' ability to identify when applicants use impression management tactics, allowing them to distinguish honest from deceptive attempts and give lower evaluations to applicants who use deception or eliminate them from the selection process. In other words, rely on Louis's ability to catch and eliminate problematic applicants. If you ask professional interviewers, and especially experienced ones like Louis, they will probably argue that they can do just that. They will most likely tell you that they can "see through" applicants and "catch" the fakers. Unfortunately, psychology research suggests a more pessimistic reality. Like Tom Hanks desperately chasing Leonardo DiCaprio in Steven Spielberg's movie, *Catch Me If You Can*, interviewers' attempts to detect when applicants use (deceptive) influence tactics is likely to be a tortuous journey.

Let's start our journey with a basic question: In general, can people accurately detect when someone is telling the truth or is lying in social situations? This question can be easily answered by looking at the large body of research on deception detection accumulated over recent decades. This research suggests that people achieve an average of about 55% correct lie-truth judgments.[35] What does this number mean? Well, imagine that you are shown a series of one hundred very short videos of individuals describing something that happened to them. After each video, you are asked a simple question: Was this story true or not? On average, people will correctly answer the question for 55 of the 100 videos, thus they are wrong for the remaining 45 videos. This may look like a reasonably good score. But consider the following alternative strategy: Instead of actually trying to detect if the story is true or not, you flip a coin after each video. If the result of the coin toss is heads, then you respond "true"; if it is tails, you respond "lie." Using the coin strategy, you will (on average) get 50 correct answers (i.e., this is what researchers call the *chance level*). So, basically, people are *not* much better than chance when it comes to deception detection. Interestingly, even individuals who detect deceit as part of their jobs (e.g., police officers, FBI agents, court judges, etc.) tend to obtain scores close to the 50% chance level on average.

Let's continue our journey with an overview of what we know about detecting deception, and influence tactics in general, in the specific context of job interviews. As described in the previous sections, the concept of influence tactics (or impression management) in interviews is more complex than the basic truth-lie distinction. An applicant can refrain from using any influence tactics, use only honest tactics, use deceptive tactics (with more or less extensive forms of deception), or use a mix of honest and deceptive tactics. As such, interviewers not only have to make a truth-or-lie assessment, they have to take into account a wide variety of tactics that candidates may be using when answering interview questions. Not surprisingly, recent studies have confirmed that detecting impression management tactics is a difficult task for interviewers. For instance, we conducted a series of studies to simulate what happens when interviewers attempt to detect influence tactics in interviews.[36] First, a number of interviews were conducted and videotaped. Candidates then watched the video of their interview and reported exactly when they used influence tactics and the type of tactics (e.g., honest vs. deceptive) used. Later, experienced professional interviewers watched excerpts of the videotaped interviews and were asked to identify in real time when an applicant was using influence tactics and the type of tactic used. The results were quite dramatic. On average, interviewers were able to correctly detect only around 20% of the tactics used by applicants. Interestingly, we replicated the study with inexperienced business and psychology students, and their performance was equivalent to the professional interviewers. Although the findings are based on a laboratory study with videotaped interviews, we obtained similar results with actual job interviews. More precisely, we conducted another study in a number of recruitment firms.[37] After the (real) interviews (for actual jobs), we took the candidates and interviewers into two separate rooms. We asked candidates to report the influence tactics they used, and we asked interviewers to report their perceptions of the tactics they thought the applicants used. We found almost no correspondence between the interviewers' perceptions and the applicants' reported behaviours.

Overall, it is quite difficult for interviewers like Louis to accurately detect whether applicants like Rachel or Kareem are using influence tactics. But can Louis be better at this task than Sonia, David, or Alice (the interviewers from the previous chapters)? The results of the interview studies presented above highlight variations in detection abilities.[38] Indeed, some interviewers' detection performance is better than chance level, whereas other interviewers perform below chance level. So it is theoretically possible for Louis to be more effective at detecting influence tactics than his colleagues (although his experience with the deceptive Eve suggests that he is certainly not flawless). Let's imagine that he is. What could make him better? Maybe he possesses a unique set of individual traits or characteristics that make him a better impression management detector. Looking at deception detection research, studies to date have failed to uncover any robust individual characteristics associated with stronger deception detection abilities.[39] In the interview context, neither age nor experience help.[40] The fact that Louis has conducted more interviews than David or Alice does not mean he performs better. An interviewer's personality profile or level of emotional intelligence does not appear to make a difference either.[41] So, for instance, Louis is not better because he is more extraverted, more conscientious, or better able to understand the emotional states of others. However, a combination of higher levels of cognitive ability and general trust may (to some extent) help interviewers be better detectors.[42] As such, Louis may outperform David or Alice because he is both more intelligent and more sensitive to whether or not an applicant is likely to be trustworthy. Yet, it is important to note that these characteristics only explain a very small part of why Louis is a better detector of influence tactics.

What really makes Louis more able to detect influence tactics is likely the way he processes information and cues provided by candidates during interviews. Contrary to other interviewers, who may follow popular beliefs about cues associated with impression management or deception, Louis might know what cues to rely on and what cues to ignore. In popular culture, liars are depicted breaking eye contact, fidgeting, or engaging in uncontrolled body movements. Many people also believe that eye movements can be used as a signal for identifying deception. For instance, believers in neuro-linguistic programming techniques think that candidates who look up and to their right are using their imagination (and thus are lying in their responses), whereas those who look to the left are using their memory (and thus are proving truthful statements). Relying on such obvious cues may be seen as an attractive (and easy) strategy for spotting deceptive applicants. However, it is not the right path to follow. In reality, those stereotypical non-verbal cues are *not* associated with deception!

There are actually very few non-verbal behaviours that can be used to tell if people are lying or to distinguish honest job candidates from deceptive ones in an interview context.[43] For instance, candidates who use deception tend to press their lips together, raise their chins more often, have more dilated pupils, or use a higher pitch when speaking. These rare valid non-verbal cues are quite subtle and difficult to identify. For example, it would probably be too difficult for Louis to determine if Kareem's or Rachel's pupils are too dilated. And these non-verbal cues are only slightly associated with deception. Interviewers would thus be better off ignoring non-verbal cues altogether. However, there are a number of valid, and possibly easier to detect, verbal cues associated with candidates' deception.[44]

Verbal cues are integrated in the candidate's discourse – that is, the content of their responses or the way the responses are formulated. For instance, liars tend to talk faster, use fewer pauses in their responses, and make more errors when speaking. Moreover, they tend to give fewer details about the experience or the context, and they describe stories that are more impersonal, more evasive, and less logically structured.[45] Altogether, Louis is a better detector because he relies on valid cues (e.g., speaking errors) and ignores stereotypical cues (e.g., gaze aversion), which helps him better distinguish whether applicants like Rachel and Kareem are describing actual or made-up qualifications or experiences.

Finally, instead of attempting the difficult task of detecting when applicants like Kareem or Rachel are faking in an interview, Louis could use strategies to prevent such behaviours from happening. For instance, some research shows that organizations can reduce applicant faking by including a warning at the start of the interview.[46] Yet, the strategy's effectiveness depends on the warning language used. Telling applicants that the organization can identify how honest or deceptive answers are (i.e., *identification* warning) seems to slightly reduce applicants' attempts to fake. In contrast, telling applicants that being truthful is the right thing to do (i.e., *moral* warning) has very little effect. Importantly, even if the former strategy demonstrates some effectiveness, as described above, generally interviewers are actually unable to detect deceptive behaviours. It thus means that organizations are actively deceiving applicants in order to reduce applicant deception. This might have some ethical (or perhaps, in some contexts, legal) implications for organizations. And, if applicants realize they have been duped, it could trigger negative reactions, like those described in Chapter 3.

Interviewers' influence tactics

Interviewers are also salespeople: Interviews as recruitment tools

In the previous section, I showed that Louis may attempt to detect when candidates like Kareem and Rachel are using impression management tactics in order to hire only the truly most qualified individuals. However, the task of assessing applicants in order to select the best ones is only one of the roles played by the interviewer. In parallel, Louis is also in a recruiting role. He is actively trying to promote the job and the organization to the applicants. Indeed, his objective is not only to select the best candidates, but also to make sure that the "chosen ones" ultimately accept an offer to join the organization.

As part of their recruitment (or salesperson) role, interviewers can impact applicants' decisions in two ways. First, they provide candidates valuable information about the job and organization. While applicants can gather information in various ways, such as via the organization's website, interviewers have the opportunity to provide more specific and targeted information, which can positively impact candidates' attraction to the job. Interviewers can try to discover what appeals to specific applicants during the interview, and then strategically signal certain aspects of the position (e.g., competitive compensation or development opportunities) or key organizational values (e.g. supportive of diversity or environmentally responsible).[47] For instance, Louis could emphasize Power Engine's focus on sustainability as a way to appeal to candidates like Rachel, who strongly values protecting the environment. In contrast, he could perhaps highlight how Power Engine uses cutting-edge technology as a strategy to be more attractive to Kareem, who emphasized his passion for novel technologies and robots.

Second, interviewers act as representatives of the organization. Because applicants often have very limited opportunities to meet the organization's other employees, they tend to use the interviewer as a prototype for what the other workers are like. Thus the interviewers' behaviour and attitudes towards applicants can project a positive image (e.g., professionalism, competence, and friendliness) or a negative image (e.g., inexperience, incompetence, and rudeness).[48] If Kareem sees Louis as a warm, funny, and competent individual, he may use this assessment to estimate that other employees at Power Engine are warm, funny, and competent. Although this is certainly a biased inference to make (i.e., other employees may well be very different from Louis), Kareem only has Louis (and perhaps a receptionist he met before the interview) as a reference point. Effective interviewers usually realize that they represent their employers and deliberately create a particular impression in applicants' minds. For instance, Louis will create a more positive impression on Kareem if he arrives on time and is well-prepared, personable, knowledgeable about the job, and able to communicate professionally.

When it comes to providing information and representing their organization, interviewers have the opportunity to truly influence applicants' perceptions about whether a job is a good fit with their qualifications and aspirations, whether they view a hiring organization as a potential place of employment, and ultimately their decision to accept a job offer.

This is how they play their part: Tactics that interviewers can use

Like job applicants, interviewers can rely on a broad range of impression management tactics to influence candidates' perceptions.[49] Interviewers can engage in self-focused tactics, similar to applicants' self-promotion, in order to enhance their competence or experience as an interviewer, their knowledge about the job and the organization, or their more personal attributes. Let's take the example of Louis's interview with Kareem. Louis can start with the following introduction:

Box 4.4

"Good morning, Kareem. My name is Louis, and I'm the HR manager here at Power Engine. I've been in the role for more than five years now, interviewing candidates among other things. In my career I have conducted more than 300 interviews."

By presenting himself and emphasizing his job title and role within the organization, Louis signals his status. He also indicates that Power Engine values Kareem and his time because he is being interviewed by the HR manager of the company, as opposed to an assistant, for instance. Moreover, by highlighting that he has extensive experience interviewing candidates, Louis demonstrates his ability to effectively assess Kareem's qualifications. In addition to demonstrating his competence and extensive knowledge about his own job, Louis could engage in other self-focused tactics – for instance, highlighting his knowledge of the engineering job that Kareem is interviewing for. This would further showcase his competence (and indirectly Power Engine employees' competence in general). He could also demonstrate humour while interacting with Kareem to signal that Power Engine employees are not only competent but also funny in order to highlight that it is an enjoyable workplace.

Beyond self-focused tactics, interviewers can engage in job-, team-, and organization-focused influence tactics.[50] Like applicants describing their qualities and accomplishments in a positive light rather than modestly, interviewers can choose to strategically emphasize the advantages associated with a particular position or the organization's recent successes. For instance, Louis could use the following description when presenting the company to Kareem:

Box 4.5

"Power Engine has been growing very quickly in the last three years. We recently became the number two engine manufacturer in the country, and we hope to become number one in the next five years. Mechanical engineers are instrumental to this success, which is why we really take care of our employees. We pay above-market salaries, offer extensive vacations, and pay for our best engineers to go to international conferences every year."

In this statement, Louis deliberately focuses on the strength of the organization and the perks associated with the engineering position. It certainly does not mean that the job and company are perfect, and there are certainly also weaknesses that Louis could have mentioned. But Louis chooses a positive framing to create a specific image in Kareem's mind – that is, one likely to make a potential job offer particularly appealing. It is important to note that interviewers can complement verbal organization-focused influence tactics with *artifactual* tactics. For instance, Louis could select and organize an interview room to create a positive impression of the organization's wealth and success – a room with expensive furniture, art on the walls, food or drinks on a table, or a beautiful view from the window signals that the company is doing well.

Just as applicants can use ingratiation tactics to create an impression of similarity or person-organization (P-O) fit, interviewers can also use similar tactics, such as praising the applicant or highlighting the applicant's fit with the organization.[51] Let's take the example of Louis's interview with Rachel. He could include the following pitch at the beginning of the interview:

Box 4.6

"Welcome, Rachel! I'm glad that you accepted our invitation to interview with Power Engine. I have to say that I was impressed by your resume. Your involvement in sustainability-related activities, like planting trees, matches the core values of our company. This is something that some of the other employees and I also try to do on a regular basis. And, your education at the Royal University and accomplishments at West Logistics are really remarkable. I can imagine you progressing through the ranks very quickly here."

In this statement, Louis uses a number of applicant-oriented (or fit-oriented) influence tactics. First, he tries to create an impression of proximity and similarity by using Rachel's first name and highlighting their shared passion for the environment. Second, he enhances the potential fit between Rachel and Power Engine by stressing how her values align with those of the company. Third, he demonstrates knowledge of Rachel's qualifications and accomplishments – for instance, by referring to her university and former employer as well as praising her experience as "remarkable." Finally, he engages in goal setting by showing a clear career path for Rachel within the organization. Of course, interviewers can also complement verbal tactics with non-verbal ones oriented towards applicants. Louis can frequently smile at Rachel, make regular eye contact, and nod when she provides answers to demonstrate interest in her as an applicant and enhance similarity. Again, Louis's verbal tactics can also be complemented with artifactual ones – for instance, a seating arrangement that creates proximity.

Before describing the potential outcomes of interviewers' impression-management tactics, I want to add three important points. First, the three broad types of tactics described above are not exclusive. Louis can decide to use one or all three of them, and he can use them at different moments (and multiple times) during the interview. For example, he could start the interview with an introduction involving self-focused tactics, follow-up with applicant-focused tactics, move on to the core questioning phase, and then conclude with job- and organization-focused tactics. Second, research suggests that the tactics interviewers use also depend on the tactics used by applicants (and vice-versa).[52] For instance, Louis could compliment Kareem's work experience right after Kareem promotes his qualifications. Or, he could emphasize sustainability as a core value of Power Engine after Rachel highlights her passion for the environment. Third, like applicants, interviewers can also engage in deceptive forms of influence tactics. For instance, Louis could exaggerate his competence or the organization's success to impress Kareem and Rachel. However, there is not yet any research exploring this side of interviewers' influence tactics. It is likely that deceived applicants will easily discover the trickery when they start working (or earlier, if they have access to other sources of information about the organization) and quicky quit the job.

Influencing applicants' decisions: Interviewers' tactics and interview outcomes

The first step towards understanding the potential impact of inter-viewers' influence tactics is to clarify the desired outcomes that the interviewer (and indirectly the organization) is trying to attain. Interviewers must be mindful of the impressions of themselves, the job, and the organization that they want to create in applicants' minds before selecting the appropriate tactics to effectively manage such impressions.[53] For instance, Louis could be trying to create an image of competence or professionalism for himself and for Power Engine in general, with the ultimate objective of making the organization attractive to candidates. Such an objective would require a specific set of self-focused and organization-focused tactics, such as highlighting his and the company's expertise, successes, or other positive attributes. Alternatively, Louis could be aiming to create an image of proximity and interest, which would produce a positive cognitive and affective state of mind in applicants like Kareem and Rachel, ultimately creating a positive connection with the organization. This would involve another constellation of influence tactics. For instance, Louis could rely on applicant-focused tactics, such as praising Kareem and Rachel, emphasizing values that he and the applicant have in common, or highlighting long-term opportunities (for personal and professional growth, promotions, etc.) within the company.

The second step is to examine research focused on the relationship between interviewers' influence tactics and actual interview outcomes, such as applicants' positive affects, ratings of an organization's attractiveness, or the likelihood a job offer will be accepted. Unfortunately, this area is still under-explored by industrial psychology researchers, and studies empirically exploring the actual outcomes of interviewers' tactics are rare. One study demonstrated that such tactics can indeed benefit the organization.[54] Interviewers who used self-focused tactics like self-promotion were perceived as more competent by job applicants, who ultimately were more attracted to the organization and more likely to accept a job offer. Moreover, interviewers who used applicant-focused tactics like ingratiation were perceived by candidates as being more interested in them, which led to positive affects towards the organization. In other words, Rachel and Kareem will be more interested in joining Power Engine if Louis engages in self-promotion and ingratiation during the interview.

There is, however, the question of asking too much of interviewers. They have to take on multiple roles, including assessing, selecting, recruiting, and attracting candidates. Each role requires cognitive resources from the interviewer. The selection role involves asking questions, attentively listening to applicants' answers, taking notes, assessing the quality of answers, ensuring that the candidate has provided enough information, identifying potential deception cues, and thinking about the next question to ask. The recruitment role involves strategically providing information and managing applicants' impressions. This is a lot to ask from interviewers, especially if they are the only person interviewing a candidate. There is a risk, therefore, that interviewers are simply not able to simultaneously effectively influence and reliably assess candidates. For instance, one study showed that when interviewers are particularly focused on "selling" the job and organization, evaluation of the candidate may suffer.[55]

Although more research is needed to fully understand how to help interviewers handle multiple roles, the safest solution is probably to encourage the use of panel interviews (as described in Chapter 2), which allows for the sharing of tasks – for instance, among a group of two or three interviewers. At Power Engine, Louis could invite a colleague to help him interview Rachel, Kareem, and the other candidates. Louis could focus on asking interview questions and evaluating the applicants, while his colleague could be in charge of engaging in influence tactics to make a good impression on the applicants (or vice-versa).

Influence tactics in job interviews: Summary

After describing how applicants and interviewers can interview effectively in Chapter 3, this chapter reviewed both tactics that Rachel and Kareem could use to influence interviewers' assessments of their qualifications and tactics that Louis could employ to influence whether applicants decide to join Power Engine. The "Toolbox" at the end of this chapter provides examples of influence tactics for applicants and interviewers as well as summaries of their potential effectiveness based on key research on the topic.[56]

Candidates can use a variety of tactics to manage interviewers' impressions, including self-promotion, ingratiation, and defensive tactics. Although Kareem and Rachel are likely to use those tactics honestly to describe their true qualifications and values, they could also decide to use them in a deceptive way – for instance, exaggerating their qualities, inventing experiences, or omitting information that could hurt their candidacy. The distinction between honest and deceptive influence tactics (or faking) is important for organizations. Indeed, if Kareem and Rachel use influence tactics (including deceptive tactics), they are likely to obtain higher ratings from Louis. This can be problematic for organizations, because they ideally want to hire candidates who actually have the right profile for the job, not those who pretend to be a good fit. Moreover, applicants who engage in faking tend to possess personality profiles (i.e., less conscientious, but more Machiavellian, Narcissistic, hyper-competitive) associated with lower work performance and a higher risk of engaging in counterproductive behaviours.

Relying on interviewers to identify and eliminate fakers is generally doomed to failure, since interviewers are largely incapable of accurately detecting influence tactics (although there may be exceptions). This is largely due to interviewers' reliance on the wrong cues to detect deception – for instance, focusing on invalid non-verbal behaviours (e.g., gaze avoidance) instead of valid verbal information (e.g., level of detail). Fortunately, Louis has the opportunity to design an interview to limit (albeit not eliminate) opportunities for Kareem or Rachel to fake – for instance, by relying on the techniques described in Chapter 2, such as standardization, panels of interviewers, and behavioural questions. Yet, he also needs to keep in mind the cultural differences associated with influence tactics and the fact that attitudes towards faking vary from one region to the next.

Finally, interviewers can also use tactics to influence applicants' impressions about them, the job, and the organization. Louis can switch his selection hat for a recruitment one and use self-, job-, organization-, or applicant-focused tactics to impress Kareem and Rachel. If used appropriately, these tactics increase the likelihood that candidates will accept a job offer. However, simultaneously wearing selection and recruitment hats is cognitively challenging, even for the most competent interviewers, which further justifies the use of a panel to conduct interviews.

Chapter 4 – Toolbox

Influence tactics applicants can use			
Honesty	**Tactic**	**What it entails**	**Goals and effectiveness**
Honest	Self-promotion	Emphasizing one's actual qualifications, skills, abilities, areas of expertise, and experiences or stressing one's individual successes or accomplishments during the interview.	Helps one appear more competent and increases perceptions of person-job fit. Strongest positive effect, especially if used in moderation.
	Ingratiation	Identifying the values, opinions, beliefs, or preferences that one shares with the interviewer and/or the values or goals that one shares with the organization and highlighting them during the interview.	Helps one appear warmer or friendlier and increases perceptions of person-organization fit. Some positive effects overall.
	Image repair	When asked about negative events or concerns in one's past, accept responsbility, provide justifications, and explain what corrective actions have been taken.	Helps defend or repair one's image as a good candidate in interviewers' minds. Some positive effects, but use only when required.
Deceptive	Image creation	Embellishing or exaggerating one's qualifications, skills, abilities, areas of expertise, experiences, or accomplishments in responses or (in extreme cases) inventing or borrowing them from others.	Attempts to appear more qualified or friendlier than one really is. Overall, unclear or limited effectiveness, although it likely varies depending on the applicant.

continued . . .

(Continued)

Honesty	Tactic	What it entails	Goals and effectiveness
	Ingratiation	Identifying the values, goals, opinions, beliefs, or preferences of the interviewer or organization and pretending during the interview that they are aligned with one's values, beliefs, etc., even when they are not.	Attempts to appear more qualified or friendlier than one really is. Overall, unclear or limited effectiveness, although it likely varies depending on the applicant.)
	Image protection	Doing everything to hide negative events or concerns in one's past or, when asked about them, denying responsibility, blaming others, or distancing oneself from the issues.	Attempts to appear more qualified or friendlier than one really is. Overall, unclear or limited effectiveness, although it likely varies depending on the applicant.)

Influence tactics interviewers can use

Tactic	What it entails	Goals and effectiveness
Self-enhancement	• Emphasizing one's skills, qualifications, or experiences as an interviewer • Highlighting one's role in the organization or in the hiring process	Creating an image of competence or professionalism, which can make the applicant feel respected and the hiring process look fairer
Job- or organization-focused enhancement	• Presenting the job in a positive way (e.g., highlighting competitive salary, benefits, growth opportunities) • Highlighting the core values and beliefs at the center of the organization's culture	Creating an image of attractiveness, which can lead to the organization being seen as more prestigious and as an employer of choice

continued . . .

(Continued)

	• Promoting the organization's brands, products, and services • Emphasizing the organization's position in the market or its business and financial successes	
Applicant enhancement	• Expressing enthusiasm about the applicant and their qualifications or flattering them • Demonstrating knowledge about the applicant, their background, experiences, etc. • Setting goals for the applicant if they decide to join the organization • Offering support to the applicant	Creating an image of closeness and building rapport, which can have positive effects on applicants' emotions, sense of self-worth, and interest in the organization
Self-, job-, or organization-focused depreciation	• Admitting one's limitations, weaknesses, or past errors • Apologizing for being late or for issues associated with the applicant's experience • Highlighting issues with the job, team, or organization	Creating an image of authenticity, which could make the interviewer or organization appear more approachable and transparent
Applicant depreciation	• Challenging or criticizing the applicant and their experiences • Downplaying the applicant's qualifications or accomplishments • Emphasizing one's status and power vs. the applicant	Creating an image of dominance or superiority, which could increase the applicant's respect or admiration for the interviewer or organization

Notes

1 Bangerter, A., N. Roulin, and C.J. König, *Personnel selection as a signaling game.* Journal of Applied Psychology, 2012. **97**(4): p. 719–738.
2 Stevens, C.K., and A.L. Kristof, *Making the right impression: A field study of applicant impression management during job interviews.* Journal of Applied

Psychology, 1995. **80**: p. 587–606; Tsai, W.-C., et al., *Disentangling the effects of applicant defensive impression management tactics in job interviews.* International Journal of Selection and Assessment, 2010. **18**: p. 131–140.

3 Stevens, C.K., and A.L. Kristof, *Making the right impression: A field study of applicant impression management during job interviews.* Journal of Applied Psychology, 1995. **80**: p. 587–606.

4 Stevens, C.K., and A.L. Kristof, *Making the right impression: A field study of applicant impression management during job interviews.* Journal of Applied Psychology, 1995. **80**: p. 587–606.

5 Kristof-Brown, A.L., M.R. Barrick, and M. Franke, *Applicant impression management: Dispositional influences and consequences for recruiter perceptions of fit and similarity.* Journal of Management, 2002. **28**: p. 27–46.

6 Stevens, C.K., and A.L. Kristof, *Making the right impression: A field study of applicant impression management during job interviews.* Journal of Applied Psychology, 1995. **80**: p. 587–606.

7 Kristof-Brown, A.L., M.R. Barrick, and M. Franke, *Applicant impression management: Dispositional influences and consequences for recruiter perceptions of fit and similarity.* Journal of Management, 2002. **28**: p. 27–46.

8 Tsai, W.-C., et al., *Disentangling the effects of applicant defensive impression management tactics in job interviews.* International Journal of Selection and Assessment, 2010. **18**: p. 131–140.

9 Stevens, C.K., and A.L. Kristof, *Making the right impression: A field study of applicant impression management during job interviews.* Journal of Applied Psychology, 1995. **80**: p. 587–606.

10 Jansen, A., et al., *Applicants' self-presentational behavior: What do recruiters expect and what do they get?* Journal of Personnel Psychology, 2012. **11**(2): p. 77–85.

11 Levashina, J., and M.A. Campion, *Measuring faking in the employment interview: Development and validation of an interview faking behavior scale.* Journal of Applied Psychology, 2007. **92**: p. 1638–1656.

12 Bourdage, J.S., N. Roulin, and R. Tarraf, *"I (might be) just that good": Honest and deceptive impression management in employment interviews.* Personnel Psychology, 2018. **71**(4): p. 597–632.

13 Weiss, B., and R.S. Feldman, *Looking good and lying to do it: Deception as an impression management strategy in job interviews.* Journal of Applied Social Psychology, 2006. **36**(4): p. 1070–1086.

14 Levashina, J., and M.A. Campion, *Measuring faking in the employment interview: Development and validation of an interview faking behavior scale.* Journal of Applied Psychology, 2007. **92**: p. 1638–1656; Bourdage, J.S., N. Roulin, and R. Tarraf, *"I (might be) just that good": Honest and deceptive impression management in employment interviews.* Personnel Psychology, 2018. **71**(4): p. 597–632.

15 Melchers, K.G., N. Roulin, and A.K. Buehl, *A review of applicant faking in selection interviews.* International Journal of Selection and Assessment, 2020. **28**(2): p. 123–142.

16 Roulin, N., F. Krings, and S. Binggeli, *A dynamic model of applicant faking.* Organizational Psychology Review, 2016. **6**(2): p. 145–170.

17 Kristof-Brown, A.L., M.R. Barrick, and M. Franke, *Applicant impression management: Dispositional influences and consequences for recruiter perceptions of fit and similarity.* Journal of Management, 2002. **28**: p. 27–46.

18 Levashina, J., and M.A. Campion, *Measuring faking in the employment interview: Development and validation of an interview faking behavior scale.* Journal of Applied Psychology, 2007. **92**: p. 1638–1656; Bourdage, J.S., N. Roulin, and R. Tarraf, *"I (might be) just that good": Honest and deceptive impression management in employment interviews.* Personnel Psychology, 2018. **71**(4): p. 597–632; Melchers, K.G., N. Roulin, and A.K. Buehl, *A review of applicant faking in selection interviews.* International Journal of Selection and Assessment, 2020. **28**(2): p. 123–142; Roulin, N., and F. Krings, *When winning is everything: The relationship between competitive worldviews and job applicant faking.* Applied Psychology: An International Review, 2016. **65**(4): p. 643–670; Roulin, N., and J.S. Bourdage, *Once an impression manager, Always an impression manager?: Antecedents of honest and deceptive impression management use and variability across multiple job interviews.* Frontiers in Psychology, 2017. **8**(29).

19 Barrick, M.R., and M.K. Mount, *The big five personality dimensions and job performance: A meta-analysis.* Personnel Psychology, 1991. **44**(1): p. 1–26; Bourdage, J.S., J. Wiltshire, and K. Lee, *Personality and impression management: Correlates and implications.* Journal of Applied Psychology, 2015. **100**(2): p. 537–546.

20 Barrick, M.R., and M.K. Mount, *The big five personality dimensions and job performance: A meta-analysis.* Personnel Psychology, 1991. **44**(1): p. 1–26.

21 Fell, C.B., C.J. König, and J. Kammerhoff, *Cross-cultural differences in the attitude toward applicants' faking in job interviews.* Journal of Business and Psychology, 2016. **31**(1): p. 65–85; Sandal, G.M., et al., *Intended self-presentation tactics in job interviews: A 10-country study.* Journal of Cross-Cultural Psychology, 2014.

22 König, C.J., J. Wong, and G. Cen, *How much do Chinese applicants fake?* International Journal of Selection and Assessment, 2012. **20**(2): p. 247–250; Husain, Z., et al., *How much self-presentation behavior do applicants from the United Arab Emirates exhibit?* International Journal of Selection and Assessment, 2018. **26**(2–4): p. 191–195.

23 Schilling, M., et al., *Do You Fake More Because of Your Neighbors?: A Multi-level Study on Regional and Individual Predictors of Faking Intentions Across the USA.* Journal of Business and Psychology, 2021. **36**: p. 193–209.

24 Ho, J.L., et al., *Willingness to fake: Examining the impact of competitive climate and hiring situations.* International Journal of Selection and Assessment, 2020. **28**(3): p. 247–263; Canagasuriam, D., and N. Roulin, The effect of organizational culture on faking in the job interview. Personnel Assessment and Decisions. 7(1): p. 8.

25 Levashina, J., et al., *The structured employment interview: Narrative and quantitative review of the research literature.* Personnel Psychology, 2014. **67**(1): p. 241–293.

26 Levashina, J., and M.A. Campion, *Measuring faking in the employment interview: Development and validation of an interview faking behavior scale.* Journal of Applied Psychology, 2007. **92**: p. 1638–1656.

27 Levashina, J., and M.A. Campion, *Measuring faking in the employment interview: Development and validation of an interview faking behavior scale.* Journal of Applied Psychology, 2007. **92**: p. 1638–1656.

28 Levashina, J., et al., *The structured employment interview: Narrative and quantitative review of the research literature.* Personnel Psychology, 2014. **67**(1): p. 241–293.

29 Bourdage, J.S., N. Roulin, and R. Tarraf, *"I (might be) just that good": Honest and deceptive impression management in employment interviews.* Personnel Psychology, 2018. **71**(4): p. 597–632.

30 Amaral, A.A., D.M. Powell, and J.L. Ho, *Why does impression management positively influence interview ratings?: The mediating role of competence and warmth.* International Journal of Selection and Assessment, 2019. **27**(4): p. 315–327.

31 Robie, C., et al., *Nonlinearity in the relationship between impression management tactics and interview performance.* International Journal of Selection and Assessment, 2020. **28**(4): p. 522–530.

32 Levashina, J., and M.A. Campion, *Measuring faking in the employment interview: Development and validation of an interview faking behavior scale.* Journal of Applied Psychology, 2007. **92**: p. 1638–1656.

33 Ho, J.L., D.M. Powell, and D.J. Stanley, *The relation between deceptive impression management and employment interview ratings: A meta-analysis.* Canadian Journal of Behavioural Science/Revue canadienne des sciences du comportement, 2021. **53**(2): p. 164–174.

34 Melchers, K.G., N. Roulin, and A.K. Buehl, *A review of applicant faking in selection interviews.* International Journal of Selection and Assessment, 2020. **28**(2): p. 123–142.

35 Bond, C.F., and B.M. DePaulo, *Accuracy of deception judgments.* Personality and Social Psychology Review, 2006. **10**(3): p. 214–234.

36 Roulin, N., A. Bangerter, and J. Levashina, *Honest and deceptive impression management in the employment interview: Can it be detected and how does it impact evaluations?* Personnel Psychology, 2015. **68**(2): p. 395–444.

37 Roulin, N., A. Bangerter, and J. Levashina, *Interviewers' perceptions of impression management in employment interviews.* Journal of Managerial Psychology, 2014. **29**(2): p. 141–163.

38 Roulin, N., A. Bangerter, and J. Levashina, *Honest and deceptive impression management in the employment interview: Can it be detected and how does it impact evaluations?* Personnel Psychology, 2015. **68**(2): p. 395–444.

39 Bond, C.F., and B.M. DePaulo, *Individual differences in judging deception: Accuracy and bias.* Psychological Bulletin, 2008. **134**(4): p. 477–492.

40 Roulin, N., A. Bangerter, and J. Levashina, *Honest and deceptive impression management in the employment interview: Can it be detected and how does it impact evaluations?* Personnel Psychology, 2015. **68**(2): p. 395–444; Roulin, N., A. Bangerter, and J. Levashina, *Interviewers' perceptions of impression management in employment interviews.* Journal of Managerial Psychology, 2014. **29**(2): p. 141–163.

41 Roulin, N., *Individual differences predicting impression management detection in job interviews.* Personnel Assessment and Decisions, 2016. **2**(1): p. 1–11; Roulin,

N., and M. Ternes, *Is it time to kill the detection wizard?: Emotional intelligence does not facilitate deception detection.* Personality and Individual Differences, 2019. **137**: p. 131–138.

42 Roulin, N., *Individual differences predicting impression management detection in job interviews.* Personnel Assessment and Decisions, 2016. **2**(1): p. 1–11.

43 DePaulo, B.M., et al., *Cues to deception.* Psychological Bulletin, 2003. **129**: p. 74–118; Schneider, L., D.M. Powell, and N. Roulin, *Cues to deception in the employment interview.* International Journal of Selection and Assessment, 2015. **23**(2): p. 182–190.

44 DePaulo, B.M., et al., *Cues to deception.* Psychological Bulletin, 2003. **129**: p. 74–118; Schneider, L., D.M. Powell, and N. Roulin, *Cues to deception in the employment interview.* International Journal of Selection and Assessment, 2015. **23**(2): p. 182–190.

45 Roulin, N., and D.M. Powell, *Identifying applicant faking in job interviews: Examining the role of criterion-based content analysis and storytelling.* Journal of Personnel Psychology, 2018. **17**(3): p. 143–154.

46 Law, S.J., J.S. Bourdage, and T.A. O'Neill, *To fake or not to fake: Antecedents to interview faking, warning instructions, and its impact on applicant reactions.* Frontiers in Psychology, 2016. **7**(1771).

47 Bangerter, A., N. Roulin, and C.J. König, *Personnel selection as a signaling game.* Journal of Applied Psychology, 2012. **97**(4): p. 719–738.

48 Wilhelmy, A., et al., *How interviewers try to make favorable impressions: A qualitative study.* Journal of Applied Psychology, 2016. **101**(3): p. 313–332.

49 Wilhelmy, A., et al., *How interviewers try to make favorable impressions: A qualitative study.* Journal of Applied Psychology, 2016. **101**(3): p. 313–332.

50 Wilhelmy, A., et al., *How interviewers try to make favorable impressions: A qualitative study.* Journal of Applied Psychology, 2016. **101**(3): p. 313–332.

51 Wilhelmy, A., et al., *How interviewers try to make favorable impressions: A qualitative study.* Journal of Applied Psychology, 2016. **101**(3): p. 313–332.

52 Wilhelmy, A., N. Roulin, and T.G. Wingate, *Does it take two to tango?: Examining how applicants and interviewers adapt their impression management to each other.* Journal of Business and Psychology, 2020.

53 Wilhelmy, A., et al., *How interviewers try to make favorable impressions: A qualitative study.* Journal of Applied Psychology, 2016. **101**(3): p. 313–332.

54 Wilhelmy, A., et al., *Selling and smooth-talking: Effects of interviewer impression management from a signaling perspective.* Frontiers in Psychology, 2017. **8**(740).

55 Marr, J.C., and D.M. Cable, *Do Interviewers Sell Themselves Short?: The Effects of Selling Orientation on Interviewers' Judgments.* Academy of Management Journal, 2014. **57**(3): p. 624–651.

56 Levashina, J., and M.A. Campion, *Measuring faking in the employment interview: Development and validation of an interview faking behavior scale.* Journal of Applied Psychology, 2007. **92**: p. 1638–1656; Bourdage, J.S., N. Roulin, and R. Tarraf, *"I (might be) just that good": Honest and deceptive impression management in employment interviews.* Personnel Psychology, 2018. **71**(4): p. 597–632; Melchers, K.G., N. Roulin, and A.K. Buehl, *A review of applicant faking in selection interviews.* International Journal of Selection and Assessment, 2020.

28(2): p. 123–142; Ho, J.L., D.M. Powell, and D.J. Stanley, *The relation between deceptive impression management and employment interview ratings: A meta-analysis.* Canadian Journal of Behavioural Science/Revue canadienne des sciences du comportement, 2021. **53**(2): p. 164–174; Wilhelmy, A., et al., *How interviewers try to make favorable impressions: A qualitative study.* Journal of Applied Psychology, 2016. **101**(3): p. 313–332; Wilhelmy, A., et al., *Selling and smooth-talking: Effects of interviewer impression management from a signaling perspective.* Frontiers in Psychology, 2017. **8**(740).

Talk to your webcam

Technology and interviewing

Rise of the machines: The role of technology in the interview

All the examples of situations presented in the previous chapters involved job applicants (like Rachel and Kareem) interacting with interviewers (like Sonia, David, Alice, and Louis) in the same physical location, usually the interviewer's office or a meeting room at the hiring organization. However, in practice, traditional face-to-face interviews are increasingly complemented (and in some cases completely replaced) by various forms of technology-mediated interviews. This might include virtual forms of interviews, where applicants still interact directly and in real time with interviewers. For instance, Kareem could be interviewed by David using video-conference software, such as Zoom, MS Teams, Skype, Webex, or Facetime. Or, the interview might take place completely asynchronously and without any real-time interaction with the interviewer – for instance, the applicant records their responses to interview questions on a web platform. Alice could invite Rachel to log into a platform like those developed by HireVue, Modern Hire, or Aon vidAssess to complete a digital, on-demand interview on her own.

DOI: 10.4324/9781003171089-5

It is important to understand that the use of digital interview techniques by organizations is only one example of how technology is used in the hiring process. There are many other examples of selection methods that have changed to include (or have been replaced by) more technology-intensive approaches. For instance, cybervetting and visiting candidates' social media profiles have become integral parts of the screening process for many recruiters and managers, and they can complement the assessment of resumes or cover letters.[1] Some organizations and researchers are even developing techniques to make the cybervetting process automatic and based solely on computer algorithms. Many organizations have also largely replaced paper-and-pencil selection tests with electronic ones, sometimes using unproctored online techniques that allow candidates to complete tests from their home computers or on-the-go using their smartphones.[2] Companies have developed video-based situational judgment tests, where candidates are asked to make decisions after viewing clips of simulated job-related interactions with colleagues, subordinates, or customers.[3] More recently, organizations have started to invest in the *gamification* of the selection process, introducing computer games or smartphone applications that candidates can play while allowing the organization to gather information about their abilities or decision-making strategies.[4]

Why are organizations using digital interviews?

As described in the previous chapters, there is quite extensive research evidence that traditional, face-to-face interviews work relatively well. If they are designed and conducted appropriately, they can be quite fair, be perceived positively by candidates, offer reliable assessments of applicants' qualifications, and accurately predict work performance. So why would interviewers or organizations decide to switch to digital forms of interviewing? Indeed, as the saying goes: "If it ain't broke … don't fix it." There are actually a number of reasons why organizations might decide to rely on technology in their interviewing processes and why organizations should perhaps consider it.[5] I describe the main ones below.

First of all, there are contexts in which virtual interviews can become a necessity. For instance, during the COVID-19 pandemic, social distancing rules, office closures, and travel restrictions imposed in countries around the world forced organizations to move most of their activities (including employee selection) online. At the peak of the pandemic, it would have been impossible, dangerous, or even illegal for Sonia to invite Rachel for an in-person interview, so a digital one represented the only safe alternative. Many organizations have also made long-term strategic decisions to close physical offices and switch to remote working, thus making digital interviewing part of their new business model.

Second, there are obvious financial reasons, because virtual interviews are generally much cheaper for the hiring organization. Although there are costs associated with using the software or web platform, they are usually much more reasonable than the direct or indirect costs for face-to-face interviews. For instance, organizations often pay (or reimburse) costs associated with transportation or accommodation for out-of-town (or out-of-country) applicants required to travel to meet with the interviewer. Imagine that Louis invites Kareem for a face-to-face interview, but Kareem lives in a different city. Louis's company would be expected to cover the cost of Kareem's mileage and parking (if Kareem can drive to the interview), his train or plane ticket (if it is a longer trip), or a night at a local hotel.

Third, virtual interviews offer flexibility for both the applicant and the interviewer(s). Interviews can be done from the comfort of one's home or office and without the need to travel, although both applicants and interviewers may be frustrated by network-connection problems.[6] They can be particularly effective if a candidate is located in another city or country, or if the candidate is currently employed, meaning the individual would not need to take extensive time away from their job (or take a day off). Going back to the example used above, if Kareem is already working for a company, it might be easier for him to take one or two *hours* off from work to have a video-conference interview with Louis rather than taking one or two *days* off to travel and meet Louis in person. If an organization uses asynchronous video interviews (AVIs), also known as on-demand interviews, they also offer applicants the flexibility to complete the interview *when* they want. For instance, Louis could invite Kareem and Rachel to record their responses on the company's platform within the next week. This means that Kareem could decide to complete his interview in the evening or during the weekend, thus avoiding the need to take time off from work (and perhaps without making his employer suspicious that he is looking for a new job). Or, imagine that Rachel cannot easily conduct a real-time interview in the middle of the day because she shares an apartment with several loud roommates. She could record her responses at a time when she knows they will be absent. AVIs offer similar advantages for parents in charge of young children, who might prefer to record their responses when the kids are asleep (or at school). They are also beneficial for people who work unusual hours (e.g., a nurse or security guard working night shifts might sleep during Louis's regular office hours) or those who work irregular hours (e.g., a waiter who could be called at the last minute to take an extra shift or an "on call" firefighter or surgeon), which makes it difficult to schedule an interview.

Finally, virtual interviews could help organizations in their attempts to increase diversity or inclusion in the workforce. For instance, individuals with physical disabilities can sometimes be disadvantaged in traditional face-to-face interviews. Imagine that when Louis meets Rachel for the first time for her interview, he realizes that she is in a wheelchair. Her status alone might lead Louis to form a more negative initial impression of her potential qualifications for the job (even if it is a biased view, and Rachel is a perfectly competent engineer – but more on that in Chapter 6). And, if Rachel accumulated several negative experiences involving interviewers not making job offers because of her disability, she might eventually become demotivated to apply for jobs. A digital interview might represent a preferred format for Rachel. She would not need to disclose her status at the initial interview stage, and her disability would not be visible to Louis in the virtual interview, thus it would not influence his initial impressions. Not only could that "level the playing field" and increase her chances of getting the job, knowing that the interview will be virtual could increase her motivation to apply in the first place.

However, the way that digital interviews work and their unique advantages still depend on the chosen format. In the next sections, I describe the two main types of virtual interviews: synchronous and asynchronous video interviews.

Synchronous video (or video-conference) interviews

A synchronous video interview involves a real-time interaction between an applicant and one or more interviewers using some form of video-conferencing software. This technology is not new. Organizations have been using video conferences for decades, and there is over 20 years of research on how they can be used for candidate interviews.[7] Video conferencing has become very popular in society as well over the years, first with computer-based software like Skype, and then with smartphone-based apps like FaceTime. Of course, most of us became even more familiar with this technology during the COVID-19 pandemic. Professional meetings, online courses, and virtual meetings with family and friends using platforms like Zoom, MS Teams, or Webex have become the norm. The same is true for job interviews.[8] As such, if David invites Rachel and Kareem to do synchronous video interviews (instead of a face-to-face interviews) for the position at Future Technology, they should not be too surprised by the format or technological requirements.

What do we know from research about video-conference interviews? Overall, industrial psychology researchers have found that interviewers' rating of such interviews can be more negative than ratings of face-to-face interviews.[9] There are a number of reasons for such differences.[10] First, compared to when they are in a room with a candidate, interviewers have less access to information and fewer opportunities for rapport building with video-conference interviews, which may lead them to evaluate the candidate less positively. Moreover, the technical problems, lag times, and poor connections that can occur with video-conference interviews may represent an additional source of anxiety for applicants like Kareem, who is already anxious in a traditional interview context. This may further prevent them from performing at their best. Video-conference interviews may create more anxiety, may limit the range of influence tactics available to applicants to impress interviewers, and could also create more negative reactions from applicants.[11] For instance, a study found that video-conference interviews were perceived as less fair than face-to-face interviews, largely because applicants viewed virtual interviews as more impersonal and thought that they allowed less communication

and offered fewer opportunities for demonstrating their qualifications.[12] Because video-conference interviews are popular and their
features are familiar to most candidates, Rachel and Kareem could
have particularly negative views of the process even before starting
the interview, and they might feel like they are not being given the
same chances to perform as they would have had in a face-to-face
interview.[13]

Importantly, although we know that applicants' reactions and interviewers' ratings of applicants may be more negative when using video-
conference interviews, psychology researchers have not yet examined
whether video-based interviews are more or less effective (i.e., valid
or reliable) than face-to-face interviews.[14] For example, we still ignore
whether interviewers' assessments based on video-conference interviews (or phone interviews, for that matter) predict future job performance as accurately as in-person ones. That is, we know that David
could effectively predict who among the candidates for the position at
Future Technology is the best fit when interviewing them in person
(especially if he uses the techniques described in Chapter 2). Yet, it
remains unclear whether he could also effectively predict which candidate is the best fit when using a synchronous video interview.

Asynchronous video (or on-demand) interviews

Interviewing with your webcam: How AVIs work

Over the last few years, organizations have started to rely on asynchronous video interviews (AVIs) in addition to (or instead of) in-person
or video-conference interviews. Again, the appetite for this new format has increased exponentially during the COVID-19 pandemic.
As an example, one of leading providers of AVIs, HireVue, reported
that their platform was used for over 17.5 million interviews in 2020
alone.[15] AVIs are also known as on-demand interviews because, unlike
video-conference interviews, they do not involve a real-time, synchro-
nized interaction with the interviewer or manager. Yet, the process
is quite simple: If candidates like Kareem and Rachel pass the initial

screening process, they are invited to complete an AVI on a web platform, which is sometimes managed/hosted by the hiring organization itself, but is often through external providers.[16]

For example, Alice just sent Rachel an email to congratulate her on passing the screening stage of the hiring process and provided her with a link to complete an AVI. Alice's email also gives Rachel a deadline for completing it – for instance, by the end of the week. However, Rachel can decide when and where she prefers to do the AVI. She can do it immediately or wait for the ideal moment, perhaps after school or work and at a time when she can complete it in a quiet environment. She only needs to have access to a computer, tablet, or smartphone with a camera and an internet connection. While most applicants complete their AVIs at home or in their offices, Rachel could arguably complete it in her backyard, in a park, in a coffeeshop, or at the library. Having done research on AVIs, I have seen people do them in some quite odd places (on a bed, in the bathroom, in a building hallway, etc.). When ready, Rachel simply logs into a secure online platform and, if asked, provides some basic information, like her name or the position she is applying for (although the information might also be embedded in the link she used to connect).

The interview then starts. Instead of having an interaction with Alice, Rachel is interacting only with her computer webcam or smartphone camera. Alice (or other HR experts at Brilliant Electronics) selected or prepared a series of interview questions for Rachel and all of the other candidates for the position to answer. In the majority of cases, the questions are simply written, although some organizations also provide video questions – for instance, Alice recorded herself asking the questions. Rachel simply reads a question, clicks on the record button, and provides an answer, which is recorded by the platform for later review by Alice or her colleagues.

I want to speak to a manager! The general pros and cons of AVIs

Because AVIs are brand new technology, there is only some empirical research examining this interviewing approach. Yet, a number of general advantages and drawbacks have already been highlighted.[17] On the positive side, AVIs include a number of the features associated with the best standardized interview practices discussed in Chapter 2. For instance, all candidates are asked the same questions in the same order. This helps create a fair process for all applicants and ensures that interviewers collect comparable information from all candidates. There is some preliminary evidence that AVIs can be valid predictors of job performance.[18] Unfortunately, the evidence is limited to a single study involving a small group of individuals who completed an AVI and then reported their own performance at work. This is weak evidence compared to the decades of research about the validity of in-person interviews. As described above, AVIs also offer more flexibility to both applicants (who can record their answers at any time and from anywhere) and interviewers (who can watch and assess recorded responses at any time and from anywhere). Moreover, in most cases, AVIs are not used to make final hiring decisions. Instead, they are often used as screening or initial interviews, which will be followed by an actual in-person (or video-conference) interview for the top candidates. The AVI format is therefore particularly interesting for campus recruiting, industries where there are high levels of turnover (e.g., retail, call centers, fast-food restaurants, hospitality), or organizations that regularly deal with large numbers of applications.

From a practical perspective, AVIs can also be less time-consuming. For instance, imagine that Kareem, Rachel, and six other candidates are asked to record their responses to eight questions. The company plans to invite only the two best candidates to a final on-site interview. If candidates provide responses averaging two or three minutes in length, we can easily estimate that each applicant will provide about 15 to 25 minutes of video material to review. This is substantially shorter than typical in-person screening interviews, which could easily take 30 minutes or more. In addition, if four of the candidates provide very weak answers to the first half of the questions, the interviewer or hiring manager could decide not to watch the remainder of the videos, thus saving even more time. In contrast, the interviewer or manager can watch the recorded interviews of particularly well-qualified candidates several times, if needed, which is impossible to do with in-person interviews unless they are video recorded.

However, there are also some issues with AVIs. For instance, research suggests that job applicants tend to have more generally negative reactions to AVIs compared to more traditional forms of interviews. They find them less fair, less valid, and more "creepy" or privacy-invading, which can lead to them being less attracted to the hiring organization.[19] For example, although applicants may appreciate the flexibility associated with AVIs, they may still prefer to have the opportunity to meet with representatives from the hiring organization. They may experience some frustration – for example, if they do not have the possibility of asking for clarification, or they do not see interviewers' reactions to their responses.[20] Some preliminary work that my colleagues and I have done collecting applicants' reactions to AVIs on various social media platforms (like Reddit) suggests that some people view not having the opportunity to talk with a (real) hiring manager as a signal that the organization does not care enough about candidates (i.e., them).

All of this is understandable. For instance, Rachel and Kareem might want to use some of the influence tactics described in Chapter 4 to increase their chances of impressing Louis and obtaining a job at Power Engine. But some of those tactics might be impossible or harder to implement effectively in AVIs.[21] For instance, you might remember that Kareem and Louis shared a passion for robots. If Kareem is able to spot the robot collection in Louis's office, he could use ingratiation tactics in his answers to emphasize their common interests. However, if an AVI is used, Kareem never meets with Louis or sees his robot collection, making it impossible to use this tactic. In general, all influence tactics that involve targeting the interviewer or hiring manager (e.g., highlighting similarities, praising them, laughing at their jokes) become moot in AVIs.

Other influence tactics, such as promoting one's qualifications or experiences, are still applicable in AVIs. Yet, it is more difficult for applicants to gauge whether they are effectively creating the intended impression on the interviewer. For example, in a live interview Rachel could examine Louis's reactions while she highlights her leadership skills by describing her role as the vice-president of an association of engineering students. Maybe Louis smiles, nods in appreciation, or takes notes. He could also make direct positive comments (e.g., "That is very interesting!") or negative ones (e.g., "Oh, OK, but this was only something you did as a student"), which would allow Rachel to provide follow-up information or help her refine her response strategy. However, Rachel could describe the exact same experience in an AVI, but she would not receive any feedback because she is only talking to her camera.

There might also be cultural differences in how applicants react to AVIs. For instance, a recent study of almost 645,000 actual job applicants from 46 countries who completed either a video-conference interview or an AVI showed that applicants generally liked both formats, but they slightly preferred video-conference interviews.[22] Importantly, some cultural dimensions also influenced reactions to the interview format. For example, AVIs were perceived more negatively by applicants in cultures with more uncertainty avoidance. People in countries high in uncertainty avoidance tend to do everything they can to make life as predictable and controllable as possible, thus they are generally more resistant to changes or innovations and more attached to traditions or religion. This suggests that applicants from Latin countries (e.g., Southern Europe or South America) might be slightly more reluctant to use AVIs than those from South-Asian, Anglo-Saxon, or Northern-European countries.

Similarly, some interviewers may miss the direct social interaction with candidates. For instance, as described in Chapter 4, part of Louis's role in the interview is to recruit candidates by "selling" the job and company to applicants like Rachel and Kareem. AVIs do not offer him many opportunities to do so, or at least not at this stage of the selection process. Interviewers may also not appreciate having to watch applicant videos, and they may be tempted to take shortcuts (e.g., watch only some of the responses, watch the videos while performing other tasks), which may negatively impact the quality of their assessments.

Overall, one also needs to consider that most (if not all) of the existing research on AVIs was conducted in the last five years or so. It is also possible that the negative reactions to AVIs reported in initial research are partly due to the novelty of the approach. Reactions may evolve as applicants and interviewers become more familiar with the technology. In addition, some research has shown that organizations can overturn negative reactions about AVIs if they explain to applicants how the format makes the hiring process more standardized and flexible.[23]

AVIs are not all the same: The role of design decisions

One particularly interesting characteristic of asynchronous, on-demand video interviews is that they can be designed in many different ways, which can influence candidates' experiences.[24] In other words, if

Kareem and Rachel are invited by two different organizations to complete an AVI, the process and format of each interview might be very different. Some of the differences could be due to the specific AVI platform used by the organization. For instance, some AVI providers offer options that others do not. But, more often, the HR or hiring manager makes a number of decisions about the AVI's design. Let's illustrate this with two AVI examples. Let's start with Kareem, who is invited to complete an AVI for the junior engineer position at Brilliant Electronics.

Box 5.1

After logging into the company's platform and entering his name, Kareem is provided with a page of instructions, which he reads very quickly because he is anxious to get started with the interview. Kareem thinks to himself, "I have so much time for each question. Seems straightforward. OK. Let's get to it!" He clicks on the "Start My Interview" icon. The first question appears on the screen. Kareem takes a few seconds to get his bearings and starts to read: "Please describe a time when...." Suddenly, Kareem realizes that there is a 30-second countdown timer on the page: 19 ... 18 ... 17. He quickly finishes reading the question: "... when you had to help resolve a problem between two or more colleagues or subordinates." Kareem checks the timer: 9 ... 8 ... 7. He takes a deep breath and starts thinking about previous experiences in school or when he was an intern that might correspond to the question. Before he can fully consider his response, the countdown reaches zero.

He can now see himself on the screen. The system is already recording him. Before he starts to talk, Kareem notices another countdown timer, which shows how much time he has left to record his answer: 01:55. So, Kareem understands that he was given two minutes to provide his response. He starts to get more anxious. He thinks: "Perhaps I should have read the

continued ...

cont.

initial instruction page more carefully." After taking a few extra seconds to gather his thoughts, Kareem starts talking about a group project he did in his last year in school. Two of his team members argued on a regular basis, and he had to step in to ensure the project's completion. Kareem knows it is not his best answer, but he thinks: "Good enough given the circumstances." There are fewer than ten seconds left. At this stage there is not much he can add or change. He closes his eyes and takes a deep breath. When he opens his eyes again, the countdown reaches zero.

The second question appears along with the same 30-second timer. This time Kareem quickly reads the question and starts considering his response. The countdown ends, the camera starts recording, and Kareem again has only two minutes to answer. The next four questions work exactly the same way. Kareem reaches the end of the interview: a total of six questions that took less that fifteen minutes to complete. He feels exhausted and is unsure about his performance. Everything went so fast!

Let's see another example. Rachel is invited to complete an AVI for the junior engineer position at Future Technology..

Box 5.2

Rachel logs into the platform and enters her name. She quickly reads through a page of instructions, which includes the phrases "take all the time you need" and "options to re-record." Rachel thinks to herself: "OK. That seems easy enough. Let's see how it goes!" She clicks on the "Start My Interview" icon. She sees

continued . . .

the first question written at the top of the screen, a small window with her video in the middle of the screen, and a "Start
My Recording" icon at the bottom. Rachel now understands
that she can spend as much time as she wants on that page.
She slowly starts to read the first question: "Please describe
a time when you had to complete a project under a very tight
deadline and/or with other competing tasks to perform." Rachel
starts thinking about her experiences: "Maybe something I did
with the engineering students association? That sounds OK,
but maybe it's not the best example." After a few seconds, she
recalls a project she was involved with when she worked as a
summer intern for West Logistics, which would fit this question
perfectly. She takes a few extra seconds to think about how to
best describe her experience. She also adjusts her webcam so
that it is positioned correctly, checks her clothes, and makes
sure that the lighting is good. After taking a deep breath, she
presses the "Start My Recording" icon

Rachel is still on the same page of the AVI platform. The only
difference is that a "Recording in Progress" message is now
visible, and there is a "Finish Recording" icon at the bottom of
the screen. Rachel starts talking, summarizes the West Logistics project, and provides a description of her role and the difficult deadline her team faced. After about 90 seconds, she clicks
the "Finish Recording" button. She leans back in her chair and
closes her eyes for a few seconds.

Rachel then focuses her attention back on the screen. She
sees that two new icons have appeared: one reads "Submit
This Response," and the other says "Record Another Response
for This Question." Rachel considers her options: "Well, my
answer wasn't bad, but if they give me a chance for a do-over,
maybe I could provide a better one. Perhaps, I could be more
specific when describing the outcome of the project. OK,

continued . . .

cont.

let's try again!" She clicks the second icon and re-records her answer, this time providing a more detailed description of the project and its outcomes. Her answer is a bit longer – maybe two or three minutes. When faced with the same two options – submit or re-record – Rachel feels confident that she provided a solid response, so she chooses to submit.

Rachel continues her interview and completes the other five questions. Each time, she takes a few moments to read the question and consider her response before starting to record. Although she does not use the re-recording option for every question, she does use it a couple more times when questions seemed harder or she thought her response could have been stronger. One time, her answer was interrupted by a phone call, so she stopped the initial recording and used the re-record option to start over. Overall, it took Rachel about 45 minutes to answer all six questions. While it took a bit longer than she had anticipated, and she feels a bit tired, she is also quite confident that she made a good impression!

Let's compare and contrast the AVIs that Kareem and Rachel experienced. As you probably noticed, a number of design elements differed between the two interviews. First, the two AVIs varied in the amount of preparation time allocated to candidates. Kareem was given only 30 seconds to read each question before the recording started automatically, whereas Rachel was able to take as much time as she needed. In practice, organizations or hiring managers often decide how much time applicants are given to prepare (e.g., 10 seconds, 30 seconds, one minute, unlimited). What Kareem experienced was perhaps closer to a synchronous interview, where the interviewer asks a question, and the applicant is usually expected to start answering right away (or after taking a few seconds for reflection). Yet, AVIs are still relatively novel, and some applicants might be unfamiliar or uncomfortable with the technology (or with recording themselves), which makes it more difficult to apply the effective interviewing techniques described in Chapter 3. For instance, Kareem might have found it difficult to identify the selection criteria, or the set-up might have created additional anxiety. In contrast, the unlimited preparation time offered to Rachel possibly facilitated her use of some of the effective interviewing techniques. Candidates like Rachel can use extra time to make sure that they understand the skills or abilities each question is trying to evaluate, identify work or school experiences that best highlight those qualifications, and consider how to present accomplishments in the best possible light (using the influence tactics described in Chapter 4).

Second, Kareem's responses were limited to two minutes in length, while Rachel could use as much time as she wanted. Organizations might decide to (strategically) limit the duration of responses. For instance, very limited response times (e.g., only one minute) mean that hiring managers spend less time reviewing and rating answers. However, time limits may result in less detailed responses, so managers will have less information about the applicant's qualifications. They can also pressure applicants to "pack" a lot of information in a very short response, which increases anxiety and limits the ability to use influence tactics. Alternatively, offering more time (e.g., up to four minutes) might signal that the organization expects applicants to provide very comprehensive responses. This might benefit some applicants, such as those who are talkative or have extensive work experiences and accomplishments to share. Yet, it can also be overwhelming for some individuals, who might have less to say or who feel pressured to use all of the time allocated.

Third, Rachel was able to record multiple response attempts for each question, whereas Kadeem was given only one shot. Again, Kareem's experience is arguably more similar to a live interview. Generally, an interviewer will not give applicants the chance to start over (and ignore what was said before). Yet, the big difference here is that an AVI does not offer the opportunity to probe or follow-up, which is generally possible in synchronous (in-person or video-conference) interviews. In other words, if Kareem misunderstands the question or provides an unclear or incomplete answer, the response he records is his final one. In addition, there is no option for the hiring manager to rephrase the question or probe to obtain extra information. There could also be some external element that impacts Kareem's recorded answer. For instance, there could be

noise in the background, an internet connection issue, or someone
who interrupts him. All would likely have a negative impact on his
performance as well as how he is evaluated by the hiring manager.
Although Rachel could also misunderstand the question or provide
incomplete responses, the option to re-record her answers at least
gives her the chance to consider whether an answer is appropriate
or as strong as possible. The opportunity to re-record also largely
alleviates concerns regarding technical issues or interruptions (like
the phone call Rachel received), because the applicant gets a do-
over if something happens. Some AVI platforms also allow applicants
to re-watch their responses before deciding either they are satisfied
with the recording or they want to try again, which helps them to
not only verify that responses are comprehensive and clear, but also
evaluate their non-verbal behaviours. All of this can possibly facilitate the use of influence tactics, reduce anxiety, and improve performance. That being said, organizations might also be concerned that
the more applicants re-record responses, the more content ends up
being very polished, but due to acting (and perhaps exaggerations)
rather than authenticity.

Of course, preparation time, response time, and re-recording
opportunities are only a few examples of the design elements that
organizations can change and influence applicants' experiences and
chances to perform. There are certainly others.[25] For instance, some
AVIs require applicants to answer all questions in a single uninterrupted session, whereas others can be completed in stages. In the
latter format, an applicant could decide to record responses to half of
the questions on one day and finish the interview the next day. This
might be particularly helpful for candidates who only have short
periods of time that are quiet and uninterrupted (e.g., parents of
new-born babies). While AVIs generally ask applicants to read interview questions, organizations could instead integrate audio or video
clips of an interviewer asking the questions. This could make the
AVI seem less impersonal and give applicants the impression that
they are actually talking to someone (giving them a "target" to influence). Overall, the key message is that the way an AVI is designed
creates different opportunities for applicants and impacts their reactions to the interview, their behaviour during the interview, and
their performance. Organizations should be aware of the influence

of design and consider the best options for their specific selection processes.

It is also important to note that the potential effects of AVI design elements described above are largely theoretical at this stage. Indeed, research empirically examining how design decisions actually impact applicants is only starting. Interestingly, some of our own preliminary findings suggest that the direct impact of some design elements might not be very strong. This is due, in part, to the fact that applicants differ in how (or how much) they use the opportunities provided to them. For instance, even when provided with extensive time for preparation or responses, some applicants use only a few seconds to prepare and provide short responses, whereas others use all of the preparation time offered to them and provide very detailed responses.

In addition, individual differences likely play an important role. For example, applicants who are more anxious in general (i.e., high on trait anxiety, as described in Chapter 3) might not systematically benefit from opportunities offered to them. Instead, they might experience even more anxiety because they tend to engage in maladaptive emotion-regulation strategies, and they focus more on personal deficiencies when reviewing their own past performance.[26] As such, very anxious applicants might, for instance, be more insecure about their performance after providing an initial response. They could use the option to re-record as a coping mechanism, hoping to do better in their second attempt. Yet, being particularly critical of their own performance, they could remain unconvinced by the second attempt (especially if they are able to re-watch it), thus making them even more anxious and possibly sending them into an anxiety-inducing spiral. More research needs to be conducted before we can ascertain how, when, and why different AVI designs impact different applicants.

When the robot decides: Automated assessments in AVIs

Another important technological evolution in interviewing is related to the advancement of artificial intelligence (AI) and specific tools like automatic speech recognition, machine learning, or natural language processing.[27] For instance, a number of AVI providers not only allow organizations to use their platforms to design interviews and have applicants to record their answers, they also offer a variety of tools or algorithms designed to automatically score applicants' performance, code non-verbal behaviours, or assess specific traits, such as personality. This means that, in some cases, hiring managers are provided with scores or recommendations about candidates without watching applicants' responses. While managers are generally encouraged to use these recommendations as preliminary indicators of each candidate's potential, which should be confirmed (or not) by reviewing the recordings, we can imagine a future in which the interviewer is completely replaced by a computer program. However, this robot-driven universe is not yet ready, and we need psychology researchers and programmers to work together to determine the reliability, validity, and fairness of such automatic assessments.

Preliminary evidence suggests that automated assessments of candidates' personalities (e.g., to what extent they are conscientious or extraverted) can be performed from AVI recordings.[28] But this research is still limited, and it does not (yet) suggest that AI can effectively replace more traditional forms of personality assessment, such as tests. There is also initial evidence that AI can be sexist and racist at times, largely because algorthms are dependent upon the data they are built upon.[29] For instance, if a company develops AI using video data from mostly young, white, male individuals, the algorithm might score applicants whose profiles differ (e.g., an older Black woman) more negatively. Similarly, AI based on native English speakers might determine that non-native speakers perform more poorly – for example, a speech-recognition algorithm makes more mistakes when transcribing or analyzing the responses of some applicants due to their accents.

There is also no guarantee that applicants will react positively to automated processes. Movie enthusiasts probably recognize that AI is often depicted negatively, whether your favourite reference is *The Terminator*, *The Matrix*, or *Avengers: Age of Ultron*. The few studies that examine how applicants view fully automated interview processes show rather negative reactions.[30] Automated interviews are perceived as impersonal and less fair, and applicants feel that that they are given fewer opportunities to perform. There are also similar concerns among hiring professionals regarding AI-based evaluations, which are perceived to limit social interaction with applicants, could perpetuate existing biases, and are expected to be viewed negatively by applicants.[31] In short, interviewers like Alice or Louis might prefer "the devil they know" (i.e., relying on their own judgment, despite its inherent limitations) rather than the one they do not (i.e., relying on automated, AI-based evaluations). All of this may prevent organizations from moving forward with fully automatic processes, at least for now. In addition, as with the challenge of providing applicants with some, but not too-detailed, feedback on their interview performance, which was discussed in Chapter 3, providing applicants with information about automated assessments must be done with care. Some recent research suggests that justifying the use of automated interview evaluation with too much information can backfire and accentuate applicants' concerns over privacy.[32]

We could also imagine that other technologies could complement this process in order to re-introduce some form of social interaction to please applicants. For instance, if virtual-reality (VR) technology and headsets become more accessible, organizations could envisage using VR to simulate the interview experience for applicants, instead of asking them to simply respond to their cameras in an AVI. Yet, the feasibility of combining video-recorded interviews and VR environments will depend on a number of factors, including the technology's popularity, costs, and applicants' reactions to it.

Legal considerations and technology in interviews

Because digital interviews evolve over time, and legislative changes usually take time, the laws in many countries and regions still lag behind practice. It is expected that new laws will be implemented (or updated) in the near future. Yet, there are a few examples of laws and regulations worth mentioning, which both applicants, like Rachel and Kareem, and interviewers, like Sonia or David, should be aware of.

Perhaps the most advanced piece of legislation is the General Data Protection Regulation (GDPR – see https://gdpr.eu) implemented in the European Union in 2018. The GDPR requires companies doing business (or recruiting employees) in Europe to conform to very strict regulations in terms of how they collect and store data from applicants, and how they ensure this data is protected. The GDPR is especially relevant to video-conferences that are recorded by interviewers and all forms of AVIs, because all such recordings include what GDPR labels as "personal data." For instance, all candidates must be provided with clear explanations about what data will be collected during the interview (e.g., video-recorded responses), how and where the data will be stored (e.g., with secured encryption on local servers), and how the data will be processed (e.g., by humans and/or AI-based algorithms). Applicants must provide unambiguous consent to all of these elements before organizations can collect and use their data. The legislation also specifies that organizations "must process data for the legitimate purposes specified explicitly to the data subject." This means, for example, that Louis cannot tell Kareem that his responses will be assessed only by him and later use AI to automatically score Kareem's responses. Importantly, GDPR also gives individuals a number of technology-related rights (https://gdpr.eu/tag/chapter-3). These include the right to access one's data (e.g., applicants could request a copy of any video recordings), the right to erase this data (e.g., applicants could request the deletion of their videos at the end of the selection process), and the right to not be subject to a decision based solely on automated processing (e.g., applicants could request that screening or selection decisions are not made based on AI only). Interviewers recruiting in the European Union should thus be aware of these rules when developing their interviewing process or deciding which AVI provider to work with.

In contrast, many other countries have fewer or more lenient laws. For instance, there are still no federal-level laws similar to the GDPR in the United States or Canada. But there are recent state-level efforts. For instance, in 2019 Illinois passed the Artificial Intelligence Video Interview Act. which requires employers to inform applicants before an interview if they plan to use AI to score video interviews and how the technology will be used (e.g., what will be evaluated). It is likely that similar laws will follow in other states. More generally, simply recording a video-conference interview or requiring applicants to record themselves in an AVI generally requires that the organization obtain applicants' consent, especially in the 11 U.S. states that have a "two-party" consent system for recording conversations.[33] Yet, somewhat contrary to the GDPR, the U.S. Uniform Guidelines on Employee Selection Procedures considers interview recordings part of the employment record, and thus recommends keeping them for at least a year.[34]

Overall, while providing a comprehensive overview of the laws relevant to the use of digital interviews or AI is beyond the scope of this book, the general conclusion is that there is a lot of variation between countries and even within countries. What interviewers and organizations can or cannot do, what they are required to tell applicants, and what kind of protection applicants are entitled to can vary extensively, from very specific and strict rules in some places, such as GDPR, to no rules in others. Therefore, both applicants and interviewers should make sure they are aware if such laws exist where they are interviewing and understand their impact.

Technology in interviews: Summary

Whether they like it or not, both job applicants (like Rachel and Kareem) and interviewers (like Sonia, David, Alice, and Louis) will likely face some form of technology as part of the selection process. There are many reasons to believe that technology-mediated interviews will become more and more prevalent in the near future: technological innovations like AVIs and AI-based assessments are improving, high-speed internet via home computers or smartphones is increasingly accessible, costs associated with technology usage are decreasing, short-term and project-based work (e.g., the "gig economy") are growing in importance, and remote working is becoming more common (whether due to external factors, such as the COVID-19 pandemic, or simply because organizations are trying to accommodate employees). It is therefore important that applicants and interviewers alike understand the various forms of digital interviews, their strengths and weaknesses, and how they might impact the interview process and outcomes. The "Toolbox" at the end of this chapter also presents a summary of key elements that applicants and interviewers should consider.

Overall, organizations can use either synchronous, video-conference interviews or asynchronous video interviews (AVIs). Video-conference interviews are more similar to in-person interviews, but with the flexibility of doing them from any location. The technology is arguably quite familiar to both applicants and interviewers. Yet, applicant reactions can still be slightly more negative (e.g., more impersonal, fewer opportunities to demonstrate one's qualifications), and interviewers might provide lower evaluations (e.g., because of the limited non-verbal information available or internet connection issues) as compared to traditional interviews.

AVIs represent an inexpensive and very flexible alternative, which might be particularly practical for applicants who have unusual work hours, parental responsibilities, or worries that their status could generate negative first impressions. However, generally, they are perceived even more negatively than video-conference interviews – for instance, because they do not involve social interaction with an interviewer, they provide fewer opportunities to use influence tactics, and the experience of talking to one's camera can be awkward and stressful for some individuals. Importantly, organizations can make a number of design decisions, which can change the applicants' interview experience, such as offering more preparation time, allowing longer responses, or providing opportunities for re-recording. Finally, advancements in AI technology make it possible to automate (parts of) the evaluation process.

Importantly, while there is already some research evidence about applicant reactions to and behaviours in both video-conference interviews and AVIs, we still know very little about how applicants experience AVIs with different designs, automated evaluations, or the general effectiveness of technology-mediated interviews.[35] For instance, it remains unclear how video-conference interviews or AVIs compare to in-person interviews in terms of their reliability (e.g., how consistent are evaluations from multiple interviewers, or even human interviewers vs. AI), their validity (i.e., their capacity to accurately predict future job performance or counterproductive behaviours at work), or risks of bias (e.g., towards minority applicants). Therefore, more research is needed before we can safely encourage Sonia, David, Alice, and Louis to replace traditional in-person interviews with technology-based ones, or even replace their judgments by using AI.

Chapter 5 – Toolbox

Key differences between the two forms of digital interviews		
	Video-conference interview	**AVI**
Format and process	Live interaction with one or more interviewer(s) using software, such as Zoom, Skype, MS Teams, or FaceTime	No live interaction; responses are video recorded on a web platform, such as HireVue, VidCruiter, Modern Hire or Aon vidAssess
Experience with the technology	Similar to in-person interviews; technology likely familiar to most people	Largely a novel experience for most people, although exponential growth in popularity during the COVID-19 pandemic
Structure/ design decisions	Freedom to structure and conduct the interview in ways similar to in-person interviews; most "best practices" from Chapter 2 can be applied (e.g., all applicants asked same questions in same order, panel of interviewers, standardized rating scales)	Very standardized and fair by default (i.e., all applicants asked same questions in the same order, without probing); many design options available (e.g., text vs. video questions, preparation time, response duration, re-recording, re-watching responses)
Practicality	Flexible in terms of location; cheaper/ easier to schedule than in-person interview; no travel costs for applicants; can increase accessibility (e.g., out-of-town, parents, disabled applicants)	Most flexible option; applicants can complete where and when they want; no travel costs and limited time investment can increase accessibility (e.g., out-of-town or country, parents, irregular work hours, disabled applicants)

continued . . .

(Continued)

Potential risks and technical issues	Technical issues with software; poor internet connection, webcam, or sound system	Technical issues with platform; poor internet connection (partly alleviated with re-recording or interruption options), webcam, or sound system (partly alleviated by a try-out page or practice questions)
Applicant or interviewer concerns	Limited non-verbal elements visible; limited social presence; fewer chances to perform	No probing or follow-up; no live feedback or reaction; limited non-verbal elements; no social presence or target to influence
AI use	Limited in the live interaction (unless AI-based tools are used to transcribe the interview); could be used to assess/score a recording of the interview	Can be used to obtain preliminary automated assessments of candidates based on the video (i.e., analyzing vocal or non-verbal elements) or a transcription of the responses (i.e., analyzing content for keywords or themes); offered by several AVI providers
Legal consideration for interviewers	Mostly limited to requesting applicant consent before recording a video-conference interview	Depends on local or regional laws; could involve requesting applicant consent or informing candidates how their videos will be stored and processed; might require specific explanations if AI is used
Preparation tips for applicants	Carefully check your technology (webcam, microphone, speakers or headphones, internet connection) ahead of time; select a quiet environment and neutral background; dress as if participating in a face-to-face interview	Carefully check your technology (webcam, microphone, speakers or headphones, internet connection) ahead of time; select a quiet environment and neutral background; dress as if participating in a face-to-face interview; practice speaking to a camera and recording yourself; use AVI design elements offered to you (e.g., preparation, re-recording)

Notes

1   Roulin, N., and A. Bangerter, *Social networking websites in personnel selection: A signaling perspective on recruiters' and applicants' perceptions*. Journal of Personnel Psychology, 2013. **12**(3): p. 143–151.

2   Tippins, N.T., *Where is the unproctored internet testing train headed now?* Industrial and Organizational Psychology, 2009. **2**(1): p. 69–76.

3   Lievens, F., and P.R. Sackett, *Video-based versus written situational judgment tests: A comparison in terms of predictive validity*. Journal of Applied Psychology, 2006. **91**(5): p. 1181.

4   Armstrong, M.B., R.N. Landers, and A.B. Collmus, *Gamifying Recruitment, Selection, Training, and Performance Management*, in *Emerging Research and Trends in Gamification*, H. Gangadharbatla and D.Z. Davis, Editors. 2016, IGI Global: Hershey, PA. p. 140–165.

5   Brenner, F.S., T.M. Ortner, and D. Fay, *Asynchronous video interviewing as a new technology in personnel selection: The applicant's point of view*. Frontiers in Psychology, 2016. **7**: p. 863; Lukacik, E.R., J.S. Bourdage, and N. Roulin, *Into the void: A conceptual model and research agenda for the design and use of asynchronous video interviews*. Human Resource Management Review, 2021; Torres, E.N., and C. Mejia, *Asynchronous video interviews in the hospitality industry: Considerations for virtual employee selection*. International Journal of Hospitality Management, 2017. **61**: p. 4–13.

6   Blacksmith, N., J.C. Willford, and T.S. Behrend, *Technology in the employment interview: A meta-analysis and future research agenda*. Personnel Assessment and Decisions, 2016. **2**(1): p. 12–20.

7   Blacksmith, N., J.C. Willford, and T.S. Behrend, *Technology in the employment interview: A meta-analysis and future research agenda*. Personnel Assessment and Decisions, 2016. **2**(1): p. 12–20; Chapman, D.S., and P.M. Rowe, *The influence of videoconference technology and interview structure on the recruiting function of the employment interview: A field experiment*. International Journal of Selection and Assessment, 2002. **10**(3): p. 185–197.

8   Woods, S.A., et al., *Personnel selection in the digital age: A review of validity and applicant reactions, and future research challenges*. European Journal of Work and Organizational Psychology, 2020. **29**(1): p. 64–77.

9   Van Iddekinge, C.H., et al., *Comparing the psychometric characteristics of ratings of face-to-face and videotaped structured interviews*. International Journal of Selection and Assessment, 2006. **14**(4): p. 347–359.

10 Blacksmith, N., J.C. Willford, and T.S. Behrend, *Technology in the employment interview: A meta-analysis and future research agenda*. Personnel Assessment and Decisions, 2016. **2**(1): p. 12–20.

11 Blacksmith, N., J.C. Willford, and T.S. Behrend, *Technology in the employment interview: A meta-analysis and future research agenda*. Personnel Assessment and Decisions, 2016. **2**(1): p. 12–20.

12 Basch, J.M., et al., *Smile for the camera!: The role of social presence and impression management in perceptions of technology-mediated interviews*. Journal of Managerial Psychology, 2020. **35**(4): p. 285–299.

13 Melchers, K.G., et al., *A comparison of conventional and technology-mediated selection interviews with regard to interviewees' performance, perceptions, strain, and anxiety.* Frontiers in Psychology, 2021. **11**(3851).

14 Blacksmith, N., J.C. Willford, and T.S. Behrend, *Technology in the employment interview: A meta-analysis and future research agenda.* Personnel Assessment and Decisions, 2016. **2**(1): p. 12–20.

15 HireVue, *HireVue records surge in anytime, anywhere candidate engagement.* 2020.

16 Lukacik, E.R., J.S. Bourdage, and N. Roulin, *Into the void: A conceptual model and research agenda for the design and use of asynchronous video interviews.* Human Resource Management Review, 2021.

17 Brenner, F.S., T.M. Ortner, and D. Fay, *Asynchronous video interviewing as a new technology in personnel selection: The applicant's point of view.* Frontiers in psychology, 2016. **7**: p. 863; Lukacik, E.R., J.S. Bourdage, and N. Roulin, *Into the void: A conceptual model and research agenda for the design and use of asynchronous video interviews.* Human Resource Management Review, 2021; Torres, E.N., and C. Mejia, *Asynchronous video interviews in the hospitality industry: Considerations for virtual employee selection.* International Journal of Hospitality Management, 2017. **61**: p. 4–13; Langer, M., C.J. König, and K. Krause, *Examining digital interviews for personnel selection: Applicant reactions and interviewer ratings.* International Journal of Selection and Assessment, 2017. **25**(4): p. 371–382.

18 Gorman, C.A., J. Robinson, and J.S. Gamble, *An investigation into the validity of asynchronous web-based video employment-interview ratings.* Consulting Psychology Journal: Practice and Research, 2018. **70**(2): p. 129–146.

19 Basch, J.M., et al., *Smile for the camera!: The role of social presence and impression management in perceptions of technology-mediated interviews.* Journal of Managerial Psychology, 2020. **35**(4): p. 285–299; Langer, M., C.J. König, and K. Krause, *Examining digital interviews for personnel selection: Applicant reactions and interviewer ratings.* International Journal of Selection and Assessment, 2017. **25**(4): p. 371–382; Proost, K., F. Germeys, and A. Vanderstukken, *Applicants' pre-test reactions towards video interviews: The role of expected chances to demonstrate potential and to use nonverbal cues.* European Journal of Work and Organizational Psychology, 2020: p. 1–9.

20 Blacksmith, N., J.C. Willford, and T.S. Behrend, *Technology in the employment interview: A meta-analysis and future research agenda.* Personnel Assessment and Decisions, 2016. **2**(1): p. 12–20.

21 Lukacik, E.R., J.S. Bourdage, and N. Roulin, *Into the void: A conceptual model and research agenda for the design and use of asynchronous video interviews.* Human Resource Management Review, 2021.

22 Griswold, K.R., et al., *Global differences in applicant reactions to virtual interview synchronicity.* The International Journal of Human Resource Management, 2021: p. 1–28.

23 Basch, J.M., and K.G. Melchers, *Fair and Flexible?!: Explanations can improve applicant reactions toward asynchronous video interviews.* Personnel Assessment and Decisions, 2019. **5**(3): p. 2.

24 Lukacik, E.R., J.S. Bourdage, and N. Roulin, *Into the void: A conceptual model and research agenda for the design and use of asynchronous video interviews.* Human Resource Management Review, 2021.

25 Lukacik, E.R., J.S. Bourdage, and N. Roulin, *Into the void: A conceptual model and research agenda for the design and use of asynchronous video interviews.* Human Resource Management Review, 2021.

26 Brozovich, F., and R.G. Heimberg, *An analysis of post-event processing in social anxiety disorder.* Clinical Psychology Review, 2008. **28**(6): p. 891–903.

27 Gonzalez, M.F., et al., *"Where's the IO?": Artificial intelligence and machine learning in talent management systems.* Personnel Assessment and Decisions, 2019. **5**(3): p. 5; Liem, C.C.S., et al., *Psychology Meets Machine Learning: Interdisciplinary Perspectives on Algorithmic Job Candidate Screening*, in *Explainable and Interpretable Models in Computer Vision and Machine Learning*, H.J. Escalante, et al., Editors. 2018, Springer International Publishing: Cham. p. 197–253.

28 Hickman, L., et al., *Automated video interview personality assessments: Reliability, validity, and generalizability investigations.* Journal of Applied Psychology, 2021; Hickman, L., L. Tay, and S.E. Woo, *Validity evidence for off-the-shelf language-based personality assessment using video interviews: Convergent and discriminant relationships with self and observer ratings.* Personnel Assessment and Decisions, 2019. **5**(3): p. 3.

29 Zou, J., and L. Schiebinger, *AI can be sexist and racist—it's time to make it fair.* Nature 2018. **559**: p. 324–326.

30 Langer, M., C.J. König, and M. Papathanasiou, *Highly automated job interviews: Acceptance under the influence of stakes.* International Journal of Selection and Assessment, 2019. **27**(3): p. 217–234.

31 Mirowska, A., and L. Mesnet, *Preferring the devil you know: Potential applicant reactions to artificial intelligence evaluation of interviews.* Human Resource Management Journal. DOI: 10.1111/1748-8583.12393.

32 Langer, M., et al., *Spare me the details: How the type of information about automated interviews influences applicant reactions.* International Journal of Selection and Assessment, 2021. **29**: p. 154–169.

33 Dill, J.R., *Video job interviews: Legal issues with remote access for applicants.* The National Law Review, 2020. **10**(157).

34 Grensing-Pophal, L. *How to maintain employee privacy in video interviews.* SHRM Talent Acquisition, 2020.

35 Blacksmith, N., J.C. Willford, and T.S. Behrend, *Technology in the employment interview: A meta-analysis and future research agenda.* Personnel Assessment and Decisions, 2016. **2**(1): p. 12–20; Chapman, D.S., and P.M. Rowe, *The influence of videoconference technology and interview structure on the recruiting function of the employment interview: A field experiment.* International Journal of Selection and Assessment, 2002. **10**(3): p. 185–197; Basch, J.M., et al., *Smile for the camera!: The role of social presence and impression management in perceptions of technology-mediated interviews.* Journal of Managerial Psychology, 2020. **35**(4): p. 285–299; Brenner, F.S., T.M. Ortner, and D. Fay, *Asynchronous video interviewing as a new technology in personnel selection: The applicant's point of view.* Frontiers in Psychology, 2016. **7**: p. 863; Langer, M., C.J. König, and K. Krause, *Examining digital interviews for personnel selection: Applicant reactions and interviewer ratings.* International Journal of Selection and Assessment, 2017. **25**(4): p. 371–382; Basch, J.M., and K.G. Melchers, *Fair and Flexible?!: Explanations can improve applicant reactions toward asynchronous video interviews.* Personnel Assessment and Decisions, 2019. **5**(3): p. 2; Lukacik, E.R., J.S. Bourdage, and N. Roulin, *Into the void: A conceptual model and research agenda for the design and use of asynchronous video interviews.* Human Resource Management Review, 2021.

Decision time

How to evaluate job applicants and what mistakes to avoid

The importance of decision-making in job interviews

Today, our two familiar candidates, Rachel and Kareem, are interviewing with Jennifer for a mechanical engineering position at Mechanical Design Incorporated (MDI). Jennifer is also interviewing two other candidates: Sofia and Anthony. Jennifer has an important but difficult job to do. As the gatekeeper of the organization, it is likely that her evaluation of the four candidates will have a major impact on who is offered a job and who is not. Of course, MDI may combine Jennifer's evaluations with information obtained from other selection tools, such as applicants' scores on cognitive ability tests, personality tests, or simulations. Moreover, following the interview, MDI may attempt to further verify that the chosen candidates deserve to join the organization – for instance, by engaging in reference or background checking. Yet, the interview remains the only method that is used in almost every selection process around the world, and it is often the most important factor driving hiring decisions.[1] Unless the organization obtains damaging evidence about an applicant after the interview, the individual who made the best impression during the interview is likely to be hired. Alternatively, it is usually inconceivable that an applicant

DOI: 10.4324/9781003171089-6

who failed to perform during the interview would receive a job offer. As such, Jennifer has a very important role, because she will likely decide who is worthy of joining MDI. Making a good decision can help recruit talented individuals who will contribute to the future success of the organization. Making a bad decision, however, can have extremely costly and damaging consequences.

Imagine for a minute that we have superpowers that allow us to obtain perfect information about all of the applicants. We can perfectly evaluate all four of them using the two subjective indicators of "fit," which were briefly introduced in Chapter 1.[2] This means that we know each candidate's level of person–job fit (or P-J fit) – that is, we have information about their qualifications (e.g., the skills they possess or their professional experiences) and can assess if their qualifications are sufficient to effectively perform the tasks and activities associated with the position. In parallel, we also know each applicant's level of person-organization fit (or P-O fit) – that is, we can judge if an applicant's personality, values, or aspirations make them likely to be satisfied, engaged, and loyal employees in this particular team and organization. For the sake of simplicity, let's imagine that we combine these two indicators into an overall percentage of fit. In other words, we know the extent to which each of the four applicants fits with the job requirements and the organization's culture.

For this particular job at MDI, Kareem is the most suitable candidate (let's imagine that his profile corresponds to an overall 90% fit with the job and organization). Rachel's fit is about 75%, Sofia's 60%, and Anthony's 40%. If Jennifer is able to accurately assess all four candidates' level of fit, the best possible decision would be to hire Kareem. Years of psychology research have demonstrated that individuals hired by organizations are much more likely to become happy, well-integrated, and productive employees if they possess high levels of both P-J and P-O fit. With his 90% fit, Kareem will likely become a productive employee and assimilate well in the MDI context. Because he possesses all of the necessary qualifications for the position, he is likely to quickly reach high productivity and require little training, which can represent important savings for the organization. For instance, Kareem is a team player, has outstanding analytical skills, and is very conscientious with his work. This profile is largely aligned with MDI's focus on teamwork, strict protocols, and complex approval processes for projects. Moreover, because his values and goals align with MDI's culture, he is likely to be a satisfied and committed employee who then stays longer with the organization.

Alternatively, if Jennifer is unable to accurately assess the candidates' fit and decides to hire Anthony, the outcomes could be dramatically different. Psychology research suggests that individuals who demonstrate poor P-J fit are likely to be less productive employees (at least initially), require more training to be able to perform their assigned duties, and may be let go by the organization if they fail to achieve performance objectives after the provision of additional support. Those who demonstrate poor P-O fit are also likely to feel more uncomfortable in their jobs because their values are not aligned with colleagues' values or the organizational culture, which makes them more prone to leave the organization. With his 40% fit, Anthony will likely be unable to perform his job effectively, and his lack of productivity could be costly for MDI. The organization may eventually decide to let him go after a few days or weeks, which would likely involve starting a new, costly, and time-consuming recruitment process to replace him. Or, MDI may decide to provide him with training in the hope that Anthony will eventually achieve higher performance. But training can be quite expensive, and it may take weeks (or even months) for Anthony to reach an acceptable level of productivity. Moreover, training would only solve the P-J fit problem. Anthony's values, personality, motivations, or career objectives may still not correspond with the MDI environment. For instance, Anthony may like to work independently, follow his instincts, and make rapid progress on projects, which clashes with MDI's focus on teamwork, strict protocols, and complex approval processes for projects. As a result, Anthony may experience lower motivation or job satisfaction. He may be frustrated and enter into conflicts with coworkers whose work styles do not match his own. Even if he is not fired by MDI, he may decide to leave the organization as soon as a better opportunity becomes available.

This example highlights the critical importance of hiring decisions in job interviews. Jennifer's good choices (i.e., hiring Kareem) vs. her bad ones (i.e., hiring Anthony) will have long-term consequences for MDI. It is therefore essential for interviewers to be able to accurately assess applicants' levels of fit in order to ultimately make optimal hiring decisions for their organizations. Unfortunately, industrial and organizational psychology research on interviewer decision-making has accumulated extensive empirical evidence showing that interviewers' decisions are often suboptimal.[3] For instance, Jennifer may tend to rely heavily on her subjective judgment, intuition, or "gut feeling" when assessing the four job candidates. She may believe that her extensive professional experience helps her develop a personal method for effectively evaluating applicants. This approach has three major limitations. First, the research on the subject is crystal clear: intuitive judgments in job interviews do not work. Of course, practice-based or intuitive decisions can sometimes be the correct ones. Yet, science-based or analytical decisions are correct far more often. Second, analytical decisions can be explained, justified, and reproduced. In contrast, intuitive decisions often cannot. Even when successful, an interviewer may say that they had the right intuition about a candidate, but they will have difficulties explaining the precise evaluation process that led to the decision. Finally, intuitive decisions are more often associated with various types of errors or biases as well as stereotypes, which may sometimes lead to discrimination against candidates who belong to minority or protected groups. Overall, interviewers need to be aware of potential biases in order to limit the risk that they result in poor hiring decisions.

Errors and biases in decision making ... and how to avoid them

Box 6.1

Jennifer is ready for a full day of interviewing: Rachel at 9:00 a.m., Kareem at 10:30 a.m., Sofia at 1:00 p.m., and Anthony at 2:30 p.m. She plans to spend about 60 to 70 minutes

continued . . .

cont.

> interviewing each candidate. After each interview she plans to take a few minutes to gather her thoughts and perhaps write down some notes before preparing for the next applicant. This is usual for Jennifer. As the head of the mechanical engineering department at a large company like MDI, she interviews dozens of candidates every month. Jennifer is an experienced interviewer. She has been involved in interviewing for almost a decade now, and she stopped counting the number of candidates she has interviewed a long time ago. Jennifer considers herself a competent and effective interviewer. Of course, if you ask her, she may admit that she has made some mistakes in the past, but she will argue that most of the time she has not received any complaints about her decisions. So, it seems that the colleagues and direct supervisors of new hires are usually happy with Jennifer's choices.

Were Jennifer's decisions always the optimal ones? Maybe or maybe not! Not receiving any complaints does not mean that everyone is perfectly happy with the new employees. Moreover, Jennifer may have regularly overlooked candidates who were more qualified than the ones she selected. But the problem with overlooked candidates is that they just disappear from the organization's radar as soon as they are eliminated (or not offered a job). MDI will thus never know that they could have hired better employees, and Jennifer never gets complete feedback on her applicant-selection performance. For instance, if she hires Anthony for the mechanical engineering job, MDI will never know whether Kareem would have been a better choice.

More generally, despite her extensive experience, Jennifer is like any other human being: she is prone to a series of unconscious cognitive biases when judging others. Her assessment of candidates may be influenced by initial impressions, similarity effects, halo effects, or contrast effects. These biases may impair her ability to effectively assess the true qualifications of Rachel, Kareem, Sofia, and

Anthony, and they may ultimately lead to suboptimal hiring decisions. So, what are these biases? How do they function? What can
interviewers like Jennifer do to avoid them? Let's go through them
in the next sections.

Don't be so quick to judge: First impressions and confirmation biases

You have probably already heard the following expression: "You
only get one chance to make a first impression." This is true in
many social situations: a first date, the first time you meet your
future in-laws, or your first meeting with an important client. This
adage is especially pertinent in job interviews. Research suggests
that interviewers usually form initial impressions of applicants in
the first minutes (and sometimes seconds) of an interview, and these
impressions have important effects on the rest of the interview.[4]
Interviewers tend to engage in confirmatory processes – that is, they
act in ways that help confirm their initial impressions. If the first
impression is positive, interviewers will follow-up with behaviours
that reinforce their positive assessment. For instance, they may ask
easier interview questions, spend more time "selling" the job or the
organization, and devote less time assessing the candidate's qualifications. These positive interviewer behaviours will likely elicit more
positive applicant behaviours as well. For example, candidates may
become more relaxed or provide stronger responses because the
questions are easier. In contrast, if the initial impression is negative, interviewers may ask more difficult questions, spend less time
praising the job, and provide fewer opportunities for the candidate
to change the interviewer's initial opinion. Altogether, interviewers create a self-fulfilling prophecy: they form an initial impression,
set the candidate up to respond in ways that confirm the impression, and interpret the candidate's behaviour as proof that the initial
impression was correct.[5] While applicants can try to overcome and
change a negative first impression, it is a challenging task. This is
evidenced by studies showing that interviewers' initial impressions
of applicants after the first few minutes of the interview or based on
the quality of the applicant's handshake are related to final evaluations at the end of the interview.[6]

Box 6.2

To illustrate the risks associated with first impressions, let's imagine that Rachel enters the interview room with a large smile on her face. She is very professionally dressed. She firmly shakes Jennifer's hand, compliments Jennifer's office, and praises MDI's selection process. In contrast, Kareem is more anxious and his handshake is less firm. Because he is focused on how to best answer upcoming questions, and he is nervous about his appearance (despite wearing a perfect suit), Kareem does not think of complimenting Jennifer or the organization. As a result, Rachel likely creates a great first impression in Jennifer's mind, whereas Kareem's initial impression is likely to be more negative.

It is important to note that Jennifer's initial impressions of the two candidates are based on irrelevant information (i.e., one's dress, handshake, and ability to compliment are arguably not the most pertinent factors for success in an engineer job). If Jennifer does not follow a standardized protocol (e.g., does not have a list of questions to ask every candidate or rating scales to evaluate responses), she may be unconsciously more lenient towards Rachel than Kareem – for instance, by asking her easier questions, allocating more time to describing the engineer job and MDI's culture, or giving Rachel more opportunities to ask her questions. Unless Rachel somehow struggles when answering these easier questions, Jennifer's final assessment is likely to be quite positive. In contrast, Kareem may have a tough time trying to erase his negative first impression, even if he provides excellent responses throughout the interview.

In conclusion, Rachel's chances of being offered the job will be higher than Kareem's. But, remember that Rachel's fit with the job and MDI is "only" 75%, whereas Kareem's is 90%. Hiring Rachel would not be a horrific decision, and her 75% fit is still decent (and better than Sofia's 60% or Anthony's 40%). Rachel may do an acceptable job at MDI and her manager may be satisfied with her performance. Yet, Kareem is objectively more qualified than Rachel, and he is being overlooked solely because of the negative initial impression he made, which was based on largely irrelevant factors. All in all, Jennifer's decision is still suboptimal.

So, what can Jennifer to do avoid making decisions biased by initial impressions? Most importantly, the safest approach is to ensure that she relies on a standardized process when interviewing the four candidates for the job – that is, she should follow the recommendations presented in Chapter 2, ask each candidate the same questions, and evaluate their responses using a rating scale. She should make sure that the time allocated to describing the job and the organization or responding to candidates' questions is (more or less) equivalent for all four applicants. Finally, she should be aware of the risks associated with excessive reliance on initial impressions when judging applicants. As mentioned above, Jennifer's initial gut feelings may sometimes be the right ones, but they are likely to be wrong as (if not more) often!

Attack of the clones: Looking for similarity is a risky strategy

The concept of P-O fit described above suggests that interviewers should try to select candidates with personality traits, values, and motivations that correspond to the organization's values and culture. Trying to assess P-O fit (and relying on perceived P-O fit to make hiring decisions) can sometimes be tricky, especially if the organization's culture or values are unclear or difficult to evaluate. For instance, many companies like to present themselves as "always putting customers first," "innovative," or "success driven." Although such values may be valuable from a business perspective, they can be difficult to translate into characteristics that applicants must possess. In such situations (and sometimes even when organizational values are more easily translated), interviewers may have a hard time assessing candidates' degree of P-O fit. They may be tempted to take a shortcut and use their own personality or values as a proxy for the organization's values or culture. The rationale is that an applicant who is similar to them would also be a good fit for the hiring organization. This approach may appear logical. For instance, Jennifer works for MDI, likes her job, is committed to her employers, and has excellent relationships with her coworkers and subordinates. In other words, she is a good fit with MDI. She may thus think that an applicant who is similar to her is more likely to become a happy, satisfied, and committed employee. And, psychology research confirms that interviewers tend to follow this path: perceived similarity with the applicant is associated with higher subjective assessments of P-O fit.[7]

This "similar-to-me equals a good P-O fit" approach may appear to be an easy and practical solution. There are, however, a number of issues with this strategy. First, if interviewers systematically rely on this method, the organization may end up employing an army of clones. For instance, Jennifer interviews dozens of candidates and hires two or three new employees for MDI every month. As such, if she relies on perceived similarly to assess P-O fit, the company may rapidly become populated with Jennifer-like employees. Jennifer may be a great manager and a perfect fit for her role at MDI, but Jennifer-like employees may not be the ideal individuals for other roles within the company. In addition, sometimes interviewers ask themselves: "Do I like that candidate as a person?" or "Could I work with this person?" The practical problem is that interviewers, especially HR managers, will likely not work with the hired candidate on a daily basis. As such, the question should rather be: "Could future coworkers work with the candidate?" Importantly, job candidates can use influence tactics (i.e., like those described in Chapter 4) to create an impression of similarity.[8] It is therefore possible that some candidates engage in ingratiation tactics (e.g., complimenting or praising Jennifer, pretending to share common interests with her) to inflate perceptions of similarity. Overall, hiring clones of Jennifer may be a suboptimal strategy from the organization's perspective.

Through similar-to-me approaches, interviewers also tend to favour applicants who share the same demographic characteristics as them (i.e. an effect labelled *demographic similarity* by psychology researchers).[9] Jennifer, who is a straight White female in her early forties, would thus be more likely to positively evaluate candidates who are straight, female, White, and in their thirties or forties than, for instance, an Asian woman in her fifties or a gay man in his twenties. Therefore, MDI not only risks hiring clones in terms of personality and values, but also in terms of demographics. This can have major practical implications in three key situations:

- First, employment legislation in many countries around the world protects applicants against discrimination based on factors such as gender, race, or age (among many other grounds, although what is protected varies by country, state, or region). If Jennifers only hires individuals like her, it will most certainly lead to situations where perfectly qualified applicants from minority groups are rejected, and they could sue MDI.

- Second, employment equity laws in some countries require some types of organizations to hire and employ a minimum number of workers from protected groups. For instance, Canadian organizations that are federally regulated have to employ a certain percentage of women, visible minorities, Indigenous people, and disabled individuals. If interviewers do not belong to any of these groups and they are prone to demographic similarity effects, the organization my risk not hiring enough employees from protected groups to meet federal requirements. This would have legal implications for a company like MDI.

- Finally, similarity biases may go against the organization's strategy to employ a diverse workforce. Diversity management or initiatives to improve diversity and inclusion have become very popular around the world.[10] Many social justice movements have emerged or gained in popularity over the last few years (such as Black Lives Matters and #MeToo), which has forced companies to revisit outdated or biased hiring policies. Organizations involved in such initiatives want to attract a more diverse workforce, value differences between employees (in terms of demographic characteristics, but also beliefs, values, education, etc.), and use such difference as a strategic advantage when competing against other organizations. Hiring clones would thus be detrimental to any diversity initiatives that the organization may want to implement.

The best solution for Jennifer to avoid similarly biases is, once again, to rely on a standardized process to interview the four candidates for the job. For instance, although psychology research suggests that similarity effects impact decisions when the interview lacks structure and standardization, such effects tend to disappear when a standardized approach is used.[11] For instance, using behaviour-oriented rating scales, like those presented in Chapter 2, reduces the likelihood that similar-to-me effects will bias evaluations. Using a panel composed of interviewers with diverse profiles is also a good way to reduce similarity biases, because no candidate can be similar to all of them.

But organizations can go beyond that by actively encouraging more applications from diverse candidates and by ensuring that enough diverse candidates are represented in the pool of "finalists" interviewed for the job. For instance, a recent study found that increasing the number of diverse applicants (from one to two) noticeably increases the likelihood that hiring managers will make an offer to diverse candidates.[12] Importantly, this positive effect was observed even when the second diverse candidate was objectively less qualified (i.e., acted as a "decoy"). In other words, imagine that Kareem (a qualified Black male) is competing against two candidates who are much more similar to the interviewer, Jennifer (e.g., two White male applicants named Jack and Tim). In that situation, simply adding another diverse but less-qualified candidate (e.g., an Asian male applicant named Yuan) would increase Kareem's chances of obtaining the job (and rightly so!).

Angel or demon: Halo effects and over-generalization

A job interview is usually a relatively short social interaction with only limited time for the interviewer to gather information about the applicant. At the end of the interaction, the interviewer only has a partial profile of the candidate's competencies, personality, or values. Because human beings generally dislike having such an incomplete picture, they naturally tend to "fill in the blanks" by extrapolating or inferring the missing information. It is a natural tendency, for example, to rely on beliefs that some traits or characteristics are automatically associated. In other words, an individual who possesses Trait A must logically also possess Trait B. For instance, people tend to evaluate individuals who are more physically attractive as also possessing more positive personality characteristics (e.g., being more open, extraverted, or agreeable) and as being more competent or intelligent.[13] Although it is true that more attractive individuals do possess some other valuable traits – for instance, they tend to have a greater sense of power; they tend to have a more effective non-verbal presence in social situations, like interviews; and they tend to be more intelligent – these relationships are not systematic and definitely do not guarantee that all attractive candidates are smart or qualified.[14]

During her interview with Rachel, Jennifer may have learned that the candidate is a competent negotiator because she described a past work experience in which she effectively negotiated an agreement with a supplier. However, Jennifer has no direct evidence of Rachel's active listening abilities, but she would like to have this information. She may thus infer that Rachel is also a good listener because she is a skilled negotiator. There is no guarantee, however, that those two characteristics are related, and Jennifer's inference is therefore largely speculative.

If the interviewer infers one (or several) positive characteristic(s) of the candidate based on one positive piece of information, this effect is called a *halo effect*. Like saints or angels, applicants who are the target of a halo effect are perceived as (automatically) possessing a number of positive traits. For instance, Jennifer may think that Rachel is a good listener and an excellent analyst because she is a skilled negotiatior. On the other hand, if the interviewer infers one (or several) negative characteristic(s) of the candidate based on one negative piece of information, this effect is called a *horn effect*. Like demoniac creatures, applicants who are the target of a horn effect are perceived as (automatically) possessing a number of negative traits. For instance, Jennifer may think that Kareem is unable to work under pressure and cannot deal with deadlines because he was anxious at the beginning or the interview. Yet, interview anxiety may not be a reliable signal of other key abilities, and Kareem may actually be completely able to manage pressure and deadlines.[15]

To avoid being the victim of halo or horn effects, the best approach is to make interviewers aware of their existence and encourage interviewers to avoid extrapolating information based on unrelated characteristics. Jennifer should thus not try to infer a specific quality of an applicant if she is not able to gather specific information during the interview. Not knowing if a candidate possesses an important qualification is actually less dangerous than incorrectly inferring that qualification. More generally, it is also important to realize that interviews do not allow the gathering of complete information, and interviewers are forced to make decisions based on imperfect information. It is impossible to always be correct when making hiring decisions because they are based on limited information. Interviewers must accept this unfortunate reality.[16]

Sticking out like a sore thumb: Contrast and uniqueness

First impressions, similarity, and halo effects are all biases associated with the assessment of one particular applicant. However, interviewers may also be unconsciously biased when they compare jobs applicants to each other. For instance, psychology research suggests that interviewers may be prone to *contrast effects*.[17] Such effects happen when the assessment of an applicant is influenced by the assessment of previous applicants. More precisely, the same candidate with average qualifications will be assessed more positively if they follow several unqualified candidates, but they will be assessed more negatively if the previous candidates were very qualified.

Box 6.3

Imagine that Sofia (whose qualifications are average and who has a 60% fit level) is interviewed by Jennifer after three other candidates. If those three candidates are very competent – for instance, Kareem (90% fit), Rachel (75% fit), and another candidate (85% fit) – then Sofia will appear particularly unqualified in Jennifer's eye in comparison to the other three. Jennifer may thus evaluate Sofia's fit as being closer to 45% or 50%. However, if Sofia is interviewed after Anthony (40% fit) and two other candidates (35% and 45% respectively), she may appear much more qualified, and Jennifer may rate her fit level as being closer to 70% or 75%. In summary, the same person whose fit level is objectively 60% may be perceived as being much more (i.e., 70–75%) or less (i.e., 45–50%) qualified depending on the applicants preceding her.

Such contrast effects have a limited practical impact if all candidates for the same position are interviewed one after another. Of course, the assessment of the last candidate may be slightly higher or lower, but it may not change the ranking of applicants. For instance, if Anthony is interviewed after Sofia, Rachel, and Kareem, he may be assessed as a 30% fit (instead of 40%). But that would not change the hiring decision, because Anthony would still be the least qualified (and Kareem the most qualified). Yet, because of administrative or availability reasons, organizations cannot always guarantee that all candidates will be interviewed on the same day. For instance, it is possible that two candidates will be interviewed on Monday, one on Wednesday, and one on Friday. In addition, interviewers or managers like Jennifer may also be involved in multiple selection processes at the same time.

Box 6.4

Let's imagine that, in addition to the junior engineering role that Kareem or Rachel applied for, Jennifer is also interviewing candidates for a much more senior position: a new manager for the Research and Development department at MDI. Jennifer schedules Rachel's interview for Friday at 3:00 p.m., just after interviews with three candidates for the manager position. Obviously, those three candidates will be much more experienced and competent than Rachel because they are interviewing for a higher-level role. In theory, this should not impact Rachel's chances because she is not competing against them, but against the other three junior candidates. However, because of contrast effects, Rachel's qualifications may appear weaker to Jennifer, who may unintentionally rate her lower that she deserves (e.g., rate her as a 55% fit instead of 75%).

Even if there are no objective differences in quality between applicants, interviewers' evaluations could be influenced by a *uniqueness effect*.[18] Such an effect is particularly likely to happen when interviewers rely on the popular or traditional questions described in Chapter 2 – for instance, "What is you main weakness?" or the kinds of questions found in a book about the "10 best interview questions." Such questions are so popular that most candidates can find the "best answer" in advice books or online, and they will arrive at the interview with a rehearsed answer. If Jennifer asks "What is you main weakness?" it is quite likely that Kareem, Rachel, and Sofia (who read similar books or visited similar websites) will have prepared an answer along the lines of "I am sometimes a perfectionist...." However, Anthony (who read another book) rehearsed a different response: "Sometimes I can be impatient...." The two types of answers are arguably of similar quality. Both are rather minor weaknesses, which could be interpreted rather positively (e.g., perfectionists and impatient workers can nevertheless perform well on the job). Interestingly, because it is unique, Anthony's response is likely to be evaluated more positively by Jennifer. In a study testing the uniqueness effect with different types of responses, the unique candidate was over two times more likely to receive a positive evaluation than the three non-unique candidates.[19] In this particular example, the uniqueness effect may negatively impact the quality of Jennifer's evaluations and hiring decision because Anthony is objectively the least qualified candidate.

To eliminate, or at least reduce, the risk of being biased by contrast effects, the best solution involves asking all applicants the same questions for the same position, taking notes based on their responses, and using standardized ratings scales like the ones presented in Chapter 2. The rating scales are particularly important, as they force the interviewer to assess the candidate's responses against a clear criteria for each interview question. For instance, Rachel's responses would be compared to the anchors or examples included in the scales. Jennifer would thus be able to judge the quality of Rachel's responses without using the other candidates as reference points. Moreover, to limit the risk of uniqueness effects, interviewers should shy away from popular or traditional questions, and instead use behavioural questions like those presented in Chapter 2. Such questions should be job-specific and require candidates to provide complex responses – for instance, involving the description of a past job experience. It would be very difficult for applicants to perfectly anticipate questions or prepare rehearsed answers. Furthermore, applicants will likely provide relatively dissimilar answers because they are based on different professional or personal experiences or different approaches to solving a job-related issue. As such, all responses will be relatively distinct, and a uniqueness effect (which requires one unique vs. several similar answers) will be very unlikely.

Stereotypes and discriminatory decisions ... and how to avoid them

Box 6.5

MDI's interviewer, Jennifer, is a White female in her early forties. She was born and raised in the region where she is currently working. She has a business degree. She is tall and thin, usually wears her long brown hair with a pony-tail, and is always well-dressed.

In a perfect world, all of Jennifer's characteristics and whether job applicants do (or do not) share them should not have any influence on the way she evaluates them. Indeed, candidates she interviews should ideally be assessed solely on their qualifications and the way they respond to the questions. Unfortunately, research in social and industrial or organizational psychology suggests otherwise. Oftentimes, interviewers can be influenced by explicit or implicit stereotypes – that is, generalized (and sometimes inaccurate) beliefs about the characteristics of members of a particular group. Such stereotypes can lead interviewers to stigmatize or even discriminate against candidates who belong to a particular group by evaluating them less positively.[20]

Who is likely to be stigmatized in an interview?

Jennifer is scheduled to interview Kareem, Rachel, Sofia, and Anthony today. In addition to the general biases that may affect her evaluations and decision (and described above), her assessments may also be (consciously or unconsciously) influenced by the candidates' demographic characteristics or their appearance.

Box 6.6

Let's imagine that MDI is located in London, U.K., and Jennifer was born in the London area. Our four candidates have the following profiles: Kareem is 24 years old, tall, and athletic. He was born in Lagos, Nigeria, and moved to England with his parents when he was ten. He speaks perfect English, but still has a thick Nigerian accent. Rachel is 26 years old. She was born in Lahore, Pakistan, and moved to London four years ago to study engineering. She is from a Muslim family and wears a headscarf in public. Sofia is 24 years old, short, and has long dark hair. She was born in London just after her parents immigrated from Bolivia. She has a large tribal tattoo on her neck and piercings on both ears and on her nose. Finally, Anthony is 25 years old, tall, and has short blond hair. He was born and raised in Manchester, U.K. Like Rachel, he decided to move to London to pursue his education in engineering.

None of the characteristics described above are related to requirements for the mechanical engineering job. As such, ideally, they should not influence the candidates' chances of obtaining the job at MDI. Remember, Kareem is objectively the most qualified applicant, followed by Rachel, Sofia, and Anthony. However, if we rely on the research conducted by social or organizational psychologists over recent decades, it is possible that the three more qualified candidates will be evaluated less favorably because they belong to stigmatized groups. In contrast, Anthony's chances may be higher because none of his personal or demographic characteristics are associated with any sigma in that particular context.

The groups likely to be stigmatized and discriminated against depend on the interviewer, the organization, and the region or country where the interview takes place. This is particularly true for the applicants' race, ethnicity, nationality, or immigrant status. Therefore, the groups that are considered minorities and are more prone to be victims of discrimination differ from one region to another. For instance, in the United States, African-American applicants are frequently discriminated against, and such effects are particularly strong if the interviewer are prejudiced – that is, they hold negative stereotypes against members of that group.[21] Latinos and Asian-Americans can similarly be stigmatized. In European countries, stigmatized groups are often first- or second-generation immigrants. For instance, in Belgium or the Netherlands applicants of Arab descent (or with Arab-sounding names) are often discriminated against in the selection process.[22] In Switzerland, applicants from Balkan countries (e.g., Kosovo, Albania) or Southern Europe (e.g., Spain, Italy, Portugal) are often discriminated against.[23] In the MDI context, it is therefore possible that Kareem and Rachel, who are both immigrants in the UK and display visible signs of their status (e.g., skin color, accent, scarf), will be stigmatized in their interviews.

Yet, there are also a number of groups that are victims of discrimination independently of contextual factors. For instance, plenty of evidence shows that female applicants are evaluated less positively than male applicants when applying for jobs that are perceived to be masculine, which may include management positions or jobs in engineering like the position at MDI.[24] Why? Because stereotypes about women include that they are warm and caring, but not competitive or aggressive (i.e., traits usually associated with managers) or good at maths or sciences (i.e., areas that are key for engineering positions). Although the stereotypes are not all true (e.g., actually, women are not worse at mathematics than men), and they certainly do not apply to all members of the group (e.g., some women are very competitive), they can still impact hiring decisions because interviewers tend to rely on them. In the MDI context, both Rachel and Sofia may be perceived as less competent for the job because they are women.

But women are not the only ones who can be victims of stereotypes. Senior workers are too![25] For instance, senior applicants are seen as warm (e.g., benevolent, amicable) but less competent (e.g., less effective, skilled, or trainable) than younger candidates. The warmth characteristics, although potentially positive, are usually overlooked, and interviewers may use the perceived lack of competence as a justification for their decision. The stereotypes against older applicants thus translate into lower evaluations by interviewers and lower chances of being offered a job.[26] Once again, it is important to note that older applicants (or workers) are on average as competent, skilled, and effective as younger ones. They may even possess more extensive knowledge, abilities, or experiences that could be valuable for the job. In the MDI context, all four applicants are of similar age and will thus not be impacted by the stigma associated with seniority. However, a 50-year-old candidate applying for the job could have been viewed more negatively.

There are also a number of other groups that can be stigmatized during the selection or interview process. Some of those stigmas have been discussed in psychology research for decades, whereas others have just been uncovered. The more traditional causes of stigmatization include applicants' physical attractiveness, weight, pregnancy, or disabilities.[27] For example, overweight or obese candidates are less likely to be hired than average-weight applicants with similar qualifications.[28] More recent psychology studies have explored the stigmas associated with piercings, tattoos, or smoking status. For instance, a study highlighted how applicants with facial piercings were perceived as less suitable for a job.[29] Pierced candidates were viewed as being more extraverted, but also less conscientious, less competent, or less trustworthy. As a result, pierced candidates were seen as less qualified for the position. Another series of studies described how cigarette smokers or e-cigarette vapers were assessed less positively than non-smokers.[30] For instance, smokers were perceived as being more likely to engage in counterproductive behaviours in the workplace – for instance, being late or putting less effort into their work – and thus were evaluated more negatively. Importantly, candidates with piercings or smoking habits are not necessarily less qualified for a position. In the MDI example, Sofia could be viewed more negatively because of her tattoo and piercings.

Understanding what triggers stigmatization

The personal and demographic characteristics of Kareem, Rachel, or Sofia can negatively impact how they are evaluated by Jennifer. But what is potentially going on in Jennifer's mind when she is interviewing them, and how can it influence her assessments? Although psychology researchers have developed a number of theories or models to explain this, I will rely on a recent *dual process* approach, which looks at interviewers' cognitive processes in reaction to stigmas.[31] This approach suggests that interviewers like Jennifer tend to engage in two different types of processes during their interactions with job applicants.

Type 1 processes are based on automatic heuristics – that is, mental shortcuts that people activate intuitively when facing a specific situation or piece of information. Such processes do not require a lot of attention or resources because the shortcuts have been registered in our brains through education and accumulated experiences. For instance, an experienced driver will stop at a red light without spending time or energy interpreting the information because the process – red light = stop – has been memorized and has become automatic. In the interview context, Type 1 processes involve unconscious interpretations of cues or information about the candidate, which result in instinctive emotions, thoughts, or behaviours. Like first impressions, Type 1 processes take place in the first few seconds or minutes of interacting with the applicant. For instance, Jennifer is likely to quickly notice cues about the candidates' stigmas and automatically react to those cues. She may note Kareem's skin color and Nigerian accent, Rachel's scarf and South-Asian accent, Sofia's tattoos and piercings, or Anthony's blond hair and local British accent. The stronger the cues, the easier it is for the interviewer to form an initial impression of the candidate. Skin color, grey hair, foreign accents, Muslim headscarves, and obesity are all examples of very strong cues, whereas piercings, tattoos, or wearing a Catholic cross on a necklace may sometimes be less visible and thus represent weaker cues. As such, Jennifer will quickly and easily categorize Kareem and Rachel as potential immigrants or non-nationals and Anthony as a local.

Of course, the strength and impact of intuitive reactions also depends on the interviewers' characteristics and attitudes towards various stigmas. The more Jennifer is prejudiced against immigrants or people with different origins, the more negative her reactions to Kareem and Rachel will be. Her initial assessment of their suitability for the position will likely be more negative, and (in extreme cases) she may even experience strong negative emotions towards them. The organizational culture or type of job may also play an important role. For instance, while a tribal tattoo can be associated with some undesirable characteristics, more modern types of tattoos can be seen more positively, could signal a creative personality, or could help create a younger or more "edgy" image for an employer.[32] Therefore, for a position that requires creativity (e.g., a designer) or in an organization that values creativity (e.g., an advertising agency), a tattoo may be interpreted more positively. More generally, although stigmas are usually associated with negative reactions, it is important to highlight that the same processes are also at work in cases of positive stigmas. When meeting with a physically attractive candidate or a candidate who shares characteristics with the interviewer, initial reactions and assessments will be particularly positive. For instance, Anthony's British accent suggests that he is a local, like Jennifer, which may facilitate similar-to-me effects and lead to more positive initial evaluations.

While Type 1 processes are automatic and intuitive, Type 2 processes are completely under the control of the interviewer.[33] They are conscious activities, and they require interviewers to use memory and other cognative capacities to analyze and interpret information. For instance, such processes involve analyzing and judging the quality of applicants' answers or their non-verbal behaviours. However, the initial evaluation, which is mostly driven by Type 1 processes and more prone to focus on applicants' stigmas and stereotypes, will act as an anchor. The information collected by interviewers during the course of the interview will be used to regularly adjust the initial impressions of the candidate, but final judgments will always be anchored (or influenced) by the initial impressions. Therefore, Jennifer may initially have rated (or anchored) Kareem or Rachel as unlikely to be a good fits for the engineer position at MDI. But each time they provide a good response, Jennifer should adapt her assessment of their qualifications and raise her overall evaluation of their suitability for the job. Unfortunately, because of initial impressions and confirmatory processes similar to those described in the previous sections, interviewers may sometimes be attached to their negative initial impressions, focus on information confirming that impression, and ultimately fail to to update their assessments. This is particularly true for stigmatized applicants.[34]

In addition, Type 2 processes also exist to monitor and control Type 1 impulses or behaviours, especially when such impulses could be seen as inappropriate. For example, Jennifer may have a strong opinion against visible tattoos and find them improper for employees working at MDI. When meeting Sofia, Jennifer may initially experience negative emotions (e.g., frustration or even disgust) in reaction to Sofia's neck tattoo, or she may simply be tempted to stare at the tattoo. But Jennifer knows that it would inelegant for her to openly express such emotions or glower at Sofia's tattoo during the interview. Type 2 processes are thus used to correct or control her impulses and conceal her reaction to Sofia. This impulse-control activity requires a lot of the interviewer's cognitive resources on top of the already resource-consuming core activities, such as asking questions, actively listening to and evaluating the candidate's answers, trying to judge the candidate's level of honesty, taking notes, and thinking about follow-up questions to ask. Therefore, the resources available to Jennifer to effectively adjust her initial impressions of Kareem, Rachel, or Sofia are likely to be insufficient. It will sometimes be easier to rationalize and justify the initial impressions. Overall, it may lead Jennifer to favour a non-stigmatized candidate, like Anthony, who is objectively less qualified than stigmatized candidates, like Kareem, Rachel, or Sofia. In addition to being sub-optimal from selection and business perspectives, such a decision could be detrimental to the organization from a legal standpoint – for instance, if rejected candidates sue MDI for discrimination.[35]

How can stigmatization be reduced in the interview?

What can organizations like MDI do to reduce the biases and potentially harmful effects of stigmatization in interviews? Similar to the other biases described above, the negative impact of stigmas on interviewers' evaluations can be lessened if the recommendations presented in Chapter 2 are followed. For instance, relying on a set of prepared questions to ask all applicants and evaluating applicants on standardized rating scales will help interviewers gather more comprehensive, objective, and comparable information about both stigmatized and non-stigmatized applicants. Moreover, this reduces the likelihood of exclusive reliance on anchored initial impressions (i.e., Type 1 processes), and instead creates opportunities for adjusting these impressions (i.e., Type 2 processes).[36] For instance, using this approach would ensure that Jennifer obtains equivalent information to compare the four candidates and update potential negative initial impressions about Kareem, Rachel, or Sofia.

In addition to improving the interview format and process, organizations can also work directly with interviewers to reduce stigmatization. A starting point can involve making interviewers aware of the existence of stigmas and their potentially detrimental effects.

Moreover, organizations can develop and enforce clear anti-discrimination policies and provide interviewers training about equity, diversity, and inclusion. Such training may include activities in which interviewers like Jennifer are forced to take the perspective of a stigmatized applicant, making them more aware of existing biases and unfair decisions. Such initiatives may facilitate Type 2 processes and limit or control Type 1 processes when interviewing stigmatized candidates[37] Of course, organizations should also be proactive and avoid hiring or promoting individuals who are hold strongly biased views about certain groups (e.g., racist, sexist, or otherwise prejudiced), particularly for interviewer positions.

What about biases in digital interviews?

Chapter 5 emphasized the growing popularity of technology-mediated interviews, such as video-conference or asynchronous-video interviews. Such digital forms of interviews can be more flexible and accessible, thus they can potentially contribute to increasing the diversity of the applicant pool. Yet, they can also facilitate or intensify other forms of bias, especially those associated with less-visible stigmas.[38] For instance, if MDI relies on traditional in-person interviews, Jennifer will likely interview Kareem, Rachel, Sofia, and Anthony in her office. Therefore, Jennifer's initial impressions are only influenced by visible stigmas, such as an applicant's skin color, accent, headscarf, or neck tattoo. She would not know anything about the candidate's marital or parental status, religious beliefs, sexual orientation, political preferences, or mental health. In several countries, these characteristics are also legally protected, so Jennifer would not be able to ask any questions about them. The only way for Jennifer to obtain such information would be to wait for applicants to openly disclose it. Or, she could later browse candidates' social media profiles in search of information, which is not only time-consuming, but also ethically debatable.

Let's contrast the traditional interview with a digital one. In most cases, applicants complete (or record) digital interviews from a personal space: perhaps their office at work, but most likely their home. Unless they do the interview in front of a neutral background (e.g., a white wall) or use tools to blur or virtually edit the background (which can be done with some software), the digital interview could offer interviewers more of a snapshot of who candidates are.[39] A framed family portrait or toys in the background could signal parental status. Posters, artwork, or the titles of books on a shelf could signal political preferences or social views. A cross or other religious symbol on the wall could signal religious beliefs. A picture of a same-sex partner or a rainbow flag could suggest sexual orientation. Of course, interviewers like Jennifer should be encouraged to simply ignore this information since it is generally not relevant for the job. But, as discussed above, when an applicants' backgrounds include stigma cues, they will likely be treated automatically by interviewers (via Type 1 processes) and impact initial impressions. While interviewer training might represent a short-term fix, long-term solutions for organizations might involve the use of technology, such as background blurring or automated assessments. But, as discussed in Chapter 5, there is still a lot of uncertainty surrounding the use of AI and similar tools to assess applicants.

Instead of hoping for the best, candidates are advised to be aware of the issue, check their backgrounds, and remove elements can could potentially signal personal preferences or characteristics that they wish to keep private. Even if it is unfair and arguably disappointing to have to do so, in a world that can at times appear quite divided, it might be the safer strategy to limit biases. Of course, there might be elements that applicants want to proudly display – for instance, because they are at the core of who they are. As long as applicants are aware of the risks or actually prefer to be transparent (i.e., a "take it or leave it" approach), there is certainly nothing wrong with keeping a rainbow flag on the wall or a "best mom in the world" mug on the table. Such behaviours could even be strategic and become an integral part of the set of influence tactics described in Chapter 4. To reinforce her "green" image, Rachel could make sure to clearly display her books about climate change or posters highlighting her involvement with sustainability initiatives. Kareem could display the robots he built for student competitions or perhaps science-fiction books to emphasize his "technology-oriented" profile. Yet, it is important to note that since AVI technology is relatively novel, there is still little empirical research to demonstrate how impactful candidates' background can be.

Decision-making in interviews: Summary

"With great power comes great responsibility!" This quote is probably familiar to Spider-Man fans and has been traced back to a sentence from the narrator in a 1962 issue of the *Amazing Fantasy* comic book. Similar versions of the adage are associated with historical and political figures, such as Lord Melbourne, Winston Churchill, and Franklin D. Roosevelt. Arguably, the quote is applicable to interviewers. Indeed, interviewers have the power to assess candidates and decide which one(s) should be offered a position. They can thus directly shape the future of their organization. At the same time, they have the responsibility of making the right decision. Selecting the candidate who is the most qualified or who best fits the job and organization will contribute to the company's productivity and success. In contrast, a sub-optimal hiring decision introduces an individual who may not assimilate, may require important investment or training, and could even become such a burden for the organization that the only solution is termination.

Despite having such an important responsibility, psychology research highlights that interviewers' decisions are often sub-optimal. Why? Because people in general are not excellent judges of character, and interviewers are no exception to that rule.[40] More precisely, interviewers are prone to a number of biases and errors that may impact their evaluations of job applicants. First impressions; similar-to-me, halo, horn, contrast, or uniqueness effects; and stigmatization are all important errors that can reduce the quality of interviewers' assessments. And, with the rise of digital interviews, interviewers potentially have even more information to bias their evaluations. Most of the time, interviewers like Jennifer do not deliberately engage in biased evaluations (although there can be exceptions, especially in the case of stigmatized candidates). Even the most professional and virtuous interviewer can be prone to unconscious cognitive biases. In some cases, this may also lead to discrimination against candidates from protected groups, which can be costly for the organization and hurt its image.

Fortunately, there is a (relatively) simple solution to that problem! It involves implementing the interviewing techniques described in Chapter 2. The evidence accumulated by psychology researchers is clear: such techniques can significantly reduce the risk of engaging in biases or, at least, reduce their negative impact on interviewers' evaluations. For instance, relying on a standardized interviewing process instead of an unstructured discussion with candidates will limit the effects of first impressions. Asking all applicants for the job the same behavioural interview questions will eliminate uniqueness effects. Moreover, relying on standardized rating scales to evaluate the responses to each question not only reduces the impact of halo or similarity effects, it also limits the likelihood of engaging in Type 1 processes that may hurt the chances of stigmatized applicants. If organizations also provide information and training to their interviewers, it can make them even more vigilant regarding biases and more likely to recognize the superior value of the interviewing techniques described earlier. As a result, the interviewing process will be more objective, more legally defensible, and more likely to provide the organization with qualified, motivated, and productive employees. These guidelines are also summarized the Chapter 6 "Toolbox."

In conclusion, we should not expect Jennifer to become the interviewer equivalent of Spider-Man. However, using the right interviewing techniques can help her better use her power and fulfill her responsibilities. For MDI, this would result in selecting the candidates who best fit the engineering position and MDI's culture (i.e., Kareem), while avoiding those candidates who do not fit but are favoured by cognitive biases (i.e., Anthony).

Chapter 6 – Toolbox

Type of bias/ effect	How it works	How to reduce or eliminate it
First impressions and confirmation	Interviewers form initial impressions of applicants in the first minutes of the interview based on largely irrelevant information (e.g., attractiveness, handshake), and they conduct the rest of the interview in a way that confirms such initial impressions	Force interviewers to ask all applicants for a position the same questions in the same order; use anchored rating scales to score responses to each interview question

continued . . .

(Continued)

Similar-to-me	Interviewers prefer (and rate more positively) applicants who are similar to them in terms of demographics (e.g., race, age, gender), beliefs, or preferences; can lead to discrimination or hurt diversity goals/initiatives	Use anchored rating scales to score responses to each interview question more objectively; use a panel (vs. one interviewer) and include a diverse group of interviewers on it; invite more diverse applicants to be interviewers (even as a decoy)
Halo/Horn	Interviewers assess one specific (positive or negative) characteristic of applicants, then they infer that the applicants possess a series of other (positive or negative) characteristics, even if they are not formally assessed	Create a series of interview questions specifically designed to assess job-relevant traits, skills, or abilities; assess them using anchored rating scales; train interviewers to avoid any inferences beyond job-relevant characteristics
Contrast	Interviewers' evaluations of one candidate (or their qualifications) are impacted by evaluations of other candidates who were interviewed previously; an average-quality candidate may be judged as stronger if interviewed after a group of weaker candidates (and vice-versa)	Use anchored rating scales to score responses to each interview question against objective job-related criteria (and not in comparison to other candidates)
Uniqueness	Interviewers evaluate candidates more positively if they provide unique (but not necessarily better-quality) responses	Avoid using popular interview questions that can be rehearsed; use anchored rating scales to objectively score each interview question response (and not in comparison to other candidates)

continued . . .

(Continued)

Stigmatization	Interviewers evaluate stigmatized applicants (e.g., based on race, gender, age) more negatively because stigma information (e.g., skin color, accent, grey hair) triggers automatic stereotypes; more negative initial impressions are formed, and they anchor final evaluations, despite conscious attempts to adjust judgments	Use structural elements (e.g., same questions, anchored rating scales, panel interviews) to limit the impact of initial impressions; train interviewers about stigmas and stereotypes; create and enforce anti-discrimination and pro-diversity policies

Notes

1   Huffcutt, A.I., and S.S. Culbertson, *Interviews*, in *APA Handbook of Industrial and Organizational Psychology*. 2011, American Psychological Association: Washington, D.C. p. 185–203; Steiner, D.D., *Personnel selection across the globe*, in *The Oxford Handbook of Personnel Assessment and Selection*, N. Schmitt, Editor. 2012, Oxford University Press: New York. p. 740–767.

2   Kristof-Brown, A.L., *Perceived applicant fit: Distinguishing between recruiters' perceptions of person-job and person-organization fit*. Personnel Psychology, 2000. **53**(3): p. 643–671.

3   Highhouse, S., *Stubborn reliance on intuition and subjectivity in employee selection*. Industrial and Organizational Psychology, 2008. **1**(3): p. 333–342.

4   Dougherty, T.W., D.B. Turban, and J.C. Callender, *Confirming first impressions in the employment interview: A field study of interviewer behavior*. Journal of Applied Psychology, 1994. **79**: p. 659–665.

5   Dipboye, R.L., *Self-fulfilling prophecies in the selection-recruitment interview*. The Academy of Management Review, 1982. **7**(4): p. 579–586.

6   Swider, B.W., et al., *Managing and creating an image in the interview: The role of interviewee initial impressions*. Journal of Applied Psychology, 2011. **96**(6): p. 1275–1288; Stewart, G.L., et al., *Exploring the handshake in employment interviews*. Journal of Applied Psychology, 2008. **93**: p. 1139–1146.

7   Piasentin, K.A., and D.S. Chapman, *Perceived similarity and complementarity as predictors of subjective person-organization fit*. Journal of Occupational and Organizational Psychology, 2007. **80**(2): p. 341–354.

8   Kristof-Brown, A.L., M.R. Barrick, and M. Franke, *Applicant impression management: Dispositional influences and consequences for recruiter perceptions of fit and similarity.* Journal of Management, 2002. **28**: p. 27–46.

9   McCarthy, J.M., C.H. Van Iddekinge, and M.A. Campion, *Are highly structured job interviews resistant to demographic similarity effects?* Personnel Psychology, 2010. **63**(2): p. 325–359.

10 Shen, J., et al., *Managing diversity through human resource management: An international perspective and conceptual framework.* The International Journal of Human Resource Management, 2009. **20**(2): p. 235–251.

11 McCarthy, J.M., C.H. Van Iddekinge, and M.A. Campion, *Are highly structured job interviews resistant to demographic similarity effects?* Personnel Psychology, 2010. **63**(2): p. 325–359.

12 Kuncel, N.R., and J.A. Dahlke, *Decoy effects improve diversity hiring.* Personnel Assessment and Decisions, 2020. **6**(2): p. 5.

13 Nisbett, R.E., and T.D. Wilson, *The halo effect: Evidence for unconscious alteration of judgments.* Journal of personality and social psychology, 1977. **35**(4): p. 250–256.

14 Tu, M.-H., E.K. Gilbert, and J.E. Bono, *Is beauty more than skin deep?: Attractiveness, power, and nonverbal presence in evaluations of hirability.* Personnel Psychology, 2021. DOI: 10.1111/peps.12469; Kanazawa, S., *Intelligence and physical attractiveness.* Intelligence, 2011. **39**(1): p. 7–14.

15 Schneider, L., D.M. Powell, and S. Bonaccio, *Does interview anxiety predict job performance and does it influence the predictive validity of interviews?* International Journal of Selection and Assessment, 2019. **27**(4): p. 328–336.

16 Highhouse, S., *Stubborn reliance on intuition and subjectivity in employee selection.* Industrial and Organizational Psychology, 2008. **1**(3): p. 333–342.

17 Wexley, K.N., R.E. Sanders, and G.A. Yukl, *Training interviewers to eliminate contrast effects in employment interviews.* Journal of Applied Psychology, 1973. **57**: p. 233–236.

18 Roulin, N., A. Bangerter, and E. Yerly, *The uniqueness effect in selection interviews.* Journal of Personnel Psychology, 2011. **10**(1): p. 43–47.

19 Roulin, N., A. Bangerter, and E. Yerly, *The uniqueness effect in selection interviews.* Journal of Personnel Psychology, 2011. **10**(1): p. 4–47.

20 Lee, S.Y., et al., *Discrimination in Selection Decisions: Integrating Stereotype Fit and Interdependence Theories.* Academy of Management Journal, 2015. **58**(3): p. 789–812.

21 Brief, A.P., et al., *Just doing business: Modern racism and obedience to authority as explanations for employment discrimination.* Organizational Behavior and Human Decision Processes, 2000. **81**(1): p. 72–97.

22 Derous, E., H.-H. Nguyen, and A.M. Ryan, *Hiring discrimination against Arab minorities: Interactions between prejudice and job characteristics.* Human Performance, 2009. **22**(4): p. 297–320.

23 Krings, F., and J. Olivares, *At the doorstep to employment: Discrimination against immigrants as a function of applicant ethnicity, job type, and raters' prejudice.* International Journal of Psychology, 2007. **42**(6): p. 406–417.

24 Davison, H.K., and M.J. Burke, *Sex discrimination in simulated employment contexts: A meta-analytic investigation.* Journal of Vocational Behavior, 2000. **56**(2): p. 225–248.

25 Finkelstein, L.M., and M.J. Burke, *Age stereotyping at work: The role of rater and contextual factors on evaluations of job applicants.* The Journal of General Psychology, 1998. **125**(4): p. 317–345.

26 Krings, F., S. Sczesny, and A. Kluge, *Stereotypical inferences as mediators of age discrimination: The role of competence and warmth.* British Journal of Management, 2011. **22**: p. 187–201.

27 Macan, T.H., *The employment interview: A review of current studies and directions for future research.* Human Resource Management Review, 2009. **19**(3): p. 203–218.

28 Finkelstein, L.M., R.L. Frautschy Demuth, and D.L. Sweeney, *Bias against overweight job applicants: Further explorations of when and why.* Human Resource Management, 2007. **46**(2): p. 203–222.

29 McElroy, J.C., J.K. Summers, and K. Moore, *The effect of facial piercing on perceptions of job applicants.* Organizational Behavior and Human Decision Processes, 2014. **125**(1): p. 26–38.

30 Roulin, N., and N. Bhatnagar, *Smoking as a job killer: Reactions to smokers in personnel selection.* Journal of Business Ethics, 2018. **149**(4): p. 959–972; Roulin, N., and N. Bhatnagar, *Examining the impact of applicant smoking and vaping habits in job interviews.* Human Relations, 2021. **74**(8): p. 1211–1239.

31 Derous, E., et al., *Why your stigma isn't hired: A dual-process framework of interview bias.* Human Resource Management Review, 2016. **26**: p. 90–111.

32 Burgess, M., and L. Clark, *Do the "savage origins" of tattoos cast a prejudicial shadow on contemporary tattooed individuals?* Journal of Applied Social Psychology, 2010. **40**(3): p. 746–764; Timming, A.R., *Body art as branded labour: At the intersection of employee selection and relationship marketing.* Human Relations, 2017. **70**(9): p. 1041–1063.

33 Derous, E., et al., *Why your stigma isn't hired: A dual-process framework of interview bias.* Human Resource Management Review, 2016. **26**: p. 90–111.

34 Derous, E., et al., *Why your stigma isn't hired: A dual-process framework of interview bias.* Human Resource Management Review, 2016. **26**: p. 90–111.

35 Lindsey, A., et al., *What we know and don't: Eradicating employment discrimination 50 years after the Civil Rights Act.* Industrial and Organizational Psychology, 2013. **6**(4): p. 391–413.

36 Derous, E., et al., *Why your stigma isn't hired: A dual-process framework of interview bias.* Human Resource Management Review, 2016. **26**: p. 90–111.

37 Derous, E., et al., *Why your stigma isn't hired: A dual-process framework of interview bias.* Human Resource Management Review, 2016. **26**: p. 90–111.

38 Summers, J.K., et al., *A typology of stigma within organizations: Access and treatment effects.* Journal of Organizational Behavior, 2018. **39**: p. 853–868.

39 Lukacik, E.R., J.S. Bourdage, and N. Roulin, *Into the void: A conceptual model and research agenda for the design and use of asynchronous video interviews.* Human Resource Management Review, 2021.

40 Kenny, D.A., and L. Albright, *Accuracy in interpersonal perception: A social relations analysis.* Psychological Bulletin, 1987. **102**(3): p. 390–402; Highhouse, S., *Stubborn reliance on intuition and subjectivity in employee selection.* Industrial and Organizational Psychology, 2008. **1**(3): p. 333–342.

The present and future of interviewing

The present of interviewing

In the previous chapters, we followed Rachel and Kareem (as well as other candidates like Sofia and Anthony) in their journeys to secure an engineering job and their interactions with interviewers like Sonia, David, Alice, Louis, and Jennifer. Although some portions of their rides were bumpy and others were more enjoyable, for job applicants and interviewers Rachel's and Kareem's experiences highlighted both "best practices" and errors to avoid. As such, this final chapter summarizes some key recommendations for both candidates and interviewers as well as illustrates how organizations can position the interview as a valuable long-term investment to ensure the success of their operations over time.

Five key recommendations for job applicants

If you read this book while in the process of applying for jobs (or in anticipation of doing so in the near future), you probably tried to imagine yourself in the shoes of Rachel and Kareem. Whether you are a young graduate like them or a more experienced worker, or whether you are active in engineering or another field, several key features of their adventures can be useful in your own journey. Let's focus on five key learning points.

First, your success in the interview will largely depend on your ability to identify the selection criteria (i.e., ATIC).[1] Your answers

DOI: 10.4324/9781003171089-7

to the interviewer's questions will likely be more convincing if you can "mind-read" the organization's requirements – that is, understand what construct each question is measuring. Therefore, the initial step of your journey should involve "doing your homework" before going to the interview. It is imperative to gather information about the job requirements and the organization's values and culture so you can identify the profile of the ideal person they are looking for. For instance, ask yourself the following questions: Does the job require particular technical skills (e.g., mastering software or a programming language; using equipment, machines, or technologies) or competencies (e.g., communication, negotiation, or leadership)? Does the organization value specific behaviours (e.g., initiative, creativity, teamwork) or causes (e.g., environmental sustainability, equity and diversity, the wellbeing of the local community, or other social issues)? It is important to keep in mind that the ideal profile will be unique to each application and organization, even if you apply for several jobs with similar titles. In addition to increasing your ATIC, gathering information about the job and organization will also help you set more realistic expectations about upcoming interviews.

Second, before the interview, spend some time making connections between the ideal profile's key characteristics and your own knowledge, skills, abilities, competencies, and personality. In other words, highlight your fit with the job and the organization.[2] For each connection that you are able to make, think of past experiences or accomplishments (ideally in a work context) that clearly demonstrate the required characteristics. For example, if the ideal profile involves leadership skills, identify a situation where you successfully led a group of people to achieve a positive outcome. Because you cannot perfectly anticipate all of the questions an interviewer may ask, it may be counter-productive to prepare rehearsed answers. However, you can prepare a list of pertinent past experiences to draw from during the interview when asked to demonstrate a particular skill or competency.

Third, in addition to collecting a set of experiences that can be used during the interview, you should prepare strategies for dealing with any anxiety that arises during the interaction.[3] The simplest steps include talking about your concerns with friends or family members, gathering as much information as possible about the organization, and consulting books or websites to get ready for traditional interview questions (e.g., "What is you main weakness?") in the unfortunate case that an interviewer relies on them. Alternatively, you may want to practice your interviewing skills by participating in mock interviews – for instance, ask a friend to play the role of the interviewer or take part in other types of training sessions. If your interview is digital, you can help reduce anxiety by spending time preparing and testing your technology (computer camera, microphone, internet connection), ensuring that you can complete the interview in an ideal environment (i.e., quiet space, good light, appropriate background), and practicing interviewing with the technology (e.g., do a practice video-conference interview with a friend; use practice opportunities on the AVI platform if the interview is asynchronous; and, if available on the AVI platform, use preparation or re-recording opportunities as you see fit).

Fourth, during the interview, your responses will be especially convincing if you present past experiences as stories to the interviewer. One effective way to build stories is to rely on the situation-task-action-result (or STAR) method.[4] More precisely, start by providing some contextual information (e.g., when the situation happened, the professional context, your job or role, whether you were alone or part of a team, etc.). Then, you should highlight the issue you faced, the task you had to perform, or the objective you had to reach. This should be followed by a clear description of your actual behaviours – that is, the action(s) you took to perform the task or deal with the issue. Conclude the story by emphasizing the positive outcomes that you achieved (e.g., the project was finished within the deadline, exceptional sales were achieved). Although this approach is likely to be particularly effective when interviewers ask past-behaviour-type questions, it can also be useful for illustrating responses to more general questions, such as questions based on your resume or your work preferences.

Finally, you should make sure to engage in honest impression management tactics during the interview.[5] This can involve emphasizing your qualities and accomplishments when telling your stories or highlighting similarities between your values, preferences, or personality and those of the interviewer or the organization. When used appropriately, such tactics are likely to impress the interviewer(s) and positively impact the ratings you obtain. Keep in mind, however, that these tactics can backfire if you use them too often, which could be seen as "bragging."[6] In addition, the adequate type of impression management tactics may also depend on culture. For instance, individual self-promotion is particularly expected in some cultures (e.g., in North America), whereas modesty or a focus on collective achievements is more appropriate in others (e.g., in many Asian cultures). Moreover, although applicants are sometimes motivated to engage in deceptive tactics – for instance, exaggerating their qualities or embellishing their accomplishments – such a strategy is not recommended. Deceptive tactics generally tend to be ineffective.[7] And, although faking could at times be associated with positive outcomes in the short term (e.g., increases the chance of getting the job), it can have detrimental consequences in the long term (e.g., leads to the acceptance of a job in an organization that does not really fit the candidate's profile, and the person may never properly assimilate).

Five key recommendations for interviewers

If you have been, currently are, or will be involved in conducting job interviews, you probably imagined yourself in the shoes of Sonia, David, Alice, Louis, or Jennifer while reading this book. Whether you are a professional recruiter or interviewer, an HR manager, a small business owner, or a supervisor involved in hiring future subordinates, some of the examples of interview situations described in the previous chapters may have sounded familiar to you. Let's summarize the key features of our interviewers' journeys in five key learning points.

First, if you currently go into all of your interviews with a set of favourite interview questions or questions that you found in an airport-type book about interviewing, you should probably stop doing it. Questions like "Tell me about yourself" or "What are you main strengths and weaknesses?" simply do not work. Applicants expect them, and such questions will not provide you pertinent and usable information about the applicant's ability to perform the job. Also, avoid questions related to information that is legally protected in your country (e.g., in the U.K. do not ask questions about a candidate's marital status or pregnancy). Instead, you should treat the interviewing process for each job as unique and aim to collect job-relevant information from candidates. At the end of the interview, the goal is to answer two key questions: (a) Does the candidate possess the right qualifications to perform the tasks and duties associated with the job?; and, (b) Do the candidate's values, motives, and personality match with the values and culture of the team and the organization?[8] Gathering information to assess point (a) will require different interview questions depending on the position – for instance, if you are hiring an engineer, a sales associate, a nurse, or an accountant. It is thus imperative to understand the unique requirements (e.g., knowledge, skills, abilities, or competencies) attached to each job – for instance, talk to experts in the job in question.

Second, once you have discovered the unique job requirements, make sure to develop behaviour-oriented interview questions to measure them.[9] Ideally, this involves identifying critical incidents – that is, specific work situations that can only be handled very effectively by competent employees – to illustrate adequate behaviours. Using these incidents, you can derive either past-behavioural interview questions (e.g., "Tell me about a time when you….") or situational interview questions (e.g., "Imagine that you are in the following situation … what would you do?"). The number of questions asked should align with the duration of the interview, although it should still be limited. For instance, it is safe to plan to ask six to eight questions in a one-hour interview. Note that you can use a mix of both past-behavioural and situational questions within the same interview (e.g., three of each). Because you want to obtain the most comprehensive set of information possible from each candidate, you may need to engage in probing with some of them. Therefore, it may be important to provide candidates some guidance and use the situation-task-action-result (or STAR) method to probe for additional information when needed. For instance, you could ask an applicant to provide additional contextual information or better explain the outcomes associated with a work situation.

Third, make sure that you use a standardized interviewing process for all candidates for the same position.[10] Structuring or standardizing the interview involves asking every candidate for the same job the same set of (behavioural) questions in the same order, refraining from asking different questions based on the applicant's unique resume or background, and trying to defer the candidate's questions until the end of the interview. Although such a level of standardization may be frustrating for some interviewers, it has a number of advantages. For instance, this approach significantly reduces the likelihood that unconscious biases – first impressions, similar-to-me effects, or stereotypes – will influence assessments. It thus ensures that a fair and consistent interviewing process is created for all applicants – that is, one that neither benefits some candidates nor hinders the chances of others. This can help improve applicants' reactions to you interviews, especially when combined with brief but clear explanations about the evaluation and decision-making processes and the use of behavioural questions that offer applicants opportunities to demonstrate their qualities. Standardization also offers you and your organization an extra layer of legal protection in case rejected applicants complain about their selection-process experiences. Also, keep in mind that some technological tools, such as AVIs, could allow you to quickly and effectively perform an initial applicant screening using an approach that is by default very standardized.

Fourth, take brief descriptive notes during the interview and use anchored rating scales to evaluate applicants' responses to behavioural questions.[11] Such an approach can be time-consuming at first, because developing scales is a complex task. Yet, it has numerous advantages. Importantly, you can build scales based on critical incidents collected while preparing the interview, thus better aligning your evaluations of applicants with the job requirements and your organizational context. Additionally, it reduces problems associated with recollection when conducting multiple interviews, increases the reliability of your assessments, and allows for more accurate comparisons between applicants. Using rating scales also helps you avoid automatic confirmatory processes. Instead, it forces you to engage in Type 2 processes – that is, carefully analyze and interpret the information obtained from the applicant. It is thus useful in further reducing the likelihood that biases, such as contrast or similar-to-me effects, will influence your judgments. Overall, this approach ensures that you reach a more objective hiring decision. Taking notes and using anchored rating scales is also recommended in digital interviews. While recording videos might reduce the need for note-taking, keep in mind that most countries or states/regions have laws requiring you to obtain the applicant's consent first.

Fifth, and finally, you should be aware that applicants will likely try to influence your evaluations through impression-management tactics.[12] When such tactics are honest (i.e., based on accurate information about the candidate's qualities and experiences), they will help you make a more accurate assessment of the candidate's fit with the job and organization. However, when such tactics are deceptive (i.e., candidates exaggerate their qualities or invent experiences), they may prevent you from making an informed decision. Unfortunately, even the most experienced interviewers have difficulty detecting such tactics or distinguishing honest from deceptive attempts. Trying to play the role of a detective is therefore not recommended. Yet, if you have doubts about the veracity of an applicant's statements and want to assess how truthful they are, you will be better off if you focus on the verbal information (e.g., check for errors or inconsistencies in the story) and ignore invalid non-verbal behaviours (e.g., gaze avoidance or body movements). In addition, keep in mind that you can also use impression management to influence candidates' likelihood of accepting an eventual job offer – for instance, by promoting the job and the organization or by making sure that you appear to be a warm and competent interviewer.[13]

Interviews as a long-term investment

Interviewers reading the recommendations listed above may feel overwhelmed by the amount of work required to implement them. Indeed, conducting an in-depth analysis of the job requirements and critical incidents or developing behavioural questions and anchored rating scales may appear to be a massive task. And, to be fair, it is! However, it should be considered an investment by the interviewer and the organization. This investment can be profitable over time in two ways.

In the short run, the difference between making an optimal hiring decision and an error can be extremely costly for the organization. For instance, a less competent new hire will require more training, take more time to reach an acceptable level of productivity, and, in some cases, may need to be terminated and replaced (which means starting the recruitment and selection process all over again). Rejecting more qualified candidates because of a sub-optimal interviewing process not only means missing out on potential talent for the organization, it can also lead to negative applicant reactions (which could be amplified via social media or employer reputation sites) and possibly legal issues (e.g., discrimination lawsuits). A poor decision thus represents extra work and time that must be invested by interviewers or HR professionals, and it could hurt the organization's reputation as well as have major financial repercussions.

In the long run, interviewers can recycle (some of) the material developed for one interview and re-use it in subsequent ones. More precisely, behavioural interview questions and the associated rating scales are designed to assess a particular behaviour that illustrates a skill or competency. Although some competencies are unique to a specific job, many are required for various jobs. For instance, communication can be important for jobs as diverse as sales associate, customer service representative, department manager, teacher, or physician. Of course, the type or style of communication may vary, and the interview questions and rating scales will therefore have to be slightly adapted, but the core of the material can remain similar. Therefore, the interview materials that are developed should not be hidden in a drawer at the end of the process. The organization, for example through its HR or IT department, should collect this information and make it available for future interviews. If this is done systematically, the organization could develop an electronic database of interview questions and scales associated with specific skills or competencies, which can be continuously updated over time. When the database is large enough, a manager or supervisor in charge of conducting an interview should be able to simply determine which skills are required for a specific job (or, select them from a list in the database) and automatically obtain adequate questions for interviews. Some large organizations (e.g., Google) have already implemented such a process, and interviewers can download questions and scales to a tablet or laptop computer, which they can bring to the interview. In addition to saving time and money down the line, this ensures that processes across the organization are valid, reliable, and fair.

The future of interviewing

Rachel's and Kareem's journeys depicted in the previous chapters illustrate the current state of interviewing practices. Yet, like many other social and business activities, the selection process has evolved in the last few years and is likely to evolve even more in the near future. Most importantly, the way that Sonia, David, Alice, Louis, and Jennifer interview candidates in the next decade will likely increasingly incorporate the use of technologies, it may need to consider how to respond to social movements and the call for more diversity, and it may have to align with the increasingly globalized environment surrounding their organizations.

Technology

The way that technology has radically changed how interviews are conducted around the world was extensively discussed in Chapter 5, so I will highlight only a few key points and future implications here. In summary, interviewers should consider the pros and cons of using video-conference interviews or AVIs (as well as how to optimally design AVIs).[14] There are certainly situations where digital interviews are a necessity – for instance, to protect everyone's health during a pandemic or when interviewing applicants living in other regions or countries. There are also a number of advantages associated with such interviews – for example, increasing flexibility and accessibility for applicants or reducing the cost and length of the interviewing process for organizations. Yet, the use of technology (and particularly AVIs) can limit applicants' opportunities to use impression management tactics, engage in non-verbal behaviours, and receive and interpret feedback from the interviewer. It can also increase candidates' anxiety levels. All of this might lead to more negative reactions and reduced candidate performance.

That said, we certainly need a lot more research to better understand how (and how much) different forms of technology-mediated interviews impact applicants. In addition, it is very likely that automated assessments (powered by artificial intelligence) will continue to play an increasingly important role in the interviewing process. But there is, at least at this time, still much uncertainty about the effectiveness of automated assessments (are they reliable and valid?), their legal implications (do they represent an invasion of privacy, and can they lead to biased decisions?), and users' perceptions of them (are they seen as fair by applicants and trustworthy by interviewers?).

Equity, Diversity, and Inclusion

Over the last few years, the world has experienced the emergence or re-emergence of various social movements to defend important causes, such as advancing racial justice and anti-discrimination (e.g., Black Lives Matter), reducing sexism and sexual harassment (e.g., #MeToo), protecting Indigenous cultures (e.g., decolonization), respecting LGBTQ+ rights, or dealing with climate change. In response, many organizations have taken initial steps to change the way they hire employees and manage their workforce. This has important implications for the interviewing process as well. Whereas most organizations have been mostly concerned with respecting anti-discrimination or employment equity laws, such changes will require interviewers to proactively contribute to increasing diversity in their organizations.

Some initial steps were mentioned in the previous chapters. The first step is to ensure that organizations rely on a standardized and fair interviewing process, such as described in Chapter 2. Second, organizations should try to systematically move from having one interviewer in charge of the interview process and decision to creating panels with three or more interviewers. They should also ensure that such panels include a diverse group of qualified individuals (in terms of race, gender, age, sexual orientation, disability status, etc.), and all individuals have a voice in the decision-making process. Third, interviewers should be provided extensive training about biases, stigmas or stereotypes, and other types of decision-making errors.[15] Yet, it is imperative to understand such training, including popular implicit bias training programs, is mostly useful for making interviewers aware of existing biases, but it is not a long-term solution for increasing diversity in organizations.[16] Finally, and perhaps most importantly, organizations should take the necessary measures to ensure that more diverse individuals apply for job openings in the first place – for instance, via welcoming and inclusive recruitment and communication strategies that reach out to more applicants from under-represented groups. They should also encourage processes or rules to ensure that members of such groups are represented in the pool of applicants invited for interviews. Ideally, that should mean inviting several qualified applicants from underrepresented groups or, if that is unfeasible, using the "decoy" approach described in Chapter 6.

Cross-cultural or international interviewing

Today's world is more globalized than it has ever been, and this trend is unlikely to change in the foreseeable future. People are more open to relocating in another region or country to complete their education or find work (without forgetting the political, social, and safety reasons that sometimes force people to leave their home countries). As a result, the population (and indirectly the potential pool of applicants) in many regions and large cities has become more diverse. For instance, over 40% of inhabitants in the Greater London area are non–White, while the percentage is over 55% in New York City.[17] Similarly, in the largest metropolitan areas in Canada – Toronto and Vancouver – over 45% of residents are from minority groups.[18] This means that interviewing processes in these regions will most likely involve situations in which the interviewer and the applicant have different racial, ethnic, or cultural backgrounds.

In such cases, the interviewer and the candidate may have different expectations regarding the appropriate way to conduct an interview. For example, people from more collaborative and collectivistic cultures (e.g., East-Asian countries) may initially react less positively to a very structured process focused on measuring competencies as compared to people from more individualistic and achievement-oriented cultures (e.g., Western Europe or North America).[19] Conversely, candidates from collectivistic cultures may be more open to talking about their families or hobbies – that is, topics that are usually prohibited in interviews conducted in Western cultures. Should the interviewer or organization ignore the recommendations provided above and adapt the interview to the applicant's background, ask different questions, etc.? Probably not! Why? First, because local legislation still applies. Second, and more importantly, because it would create issues associated with fairness and prevent interviewers from making accurate comparisons between candidates. Yet, it increases the necessity of providing information and guidance to all applicants before the interview, so that they know what to expect and why the organization is relying on a particular approach. Situations where the interviewer is local and the applicant is from a minority group also increase the risk of an interviewer's assessments being influenced by stigmas and stereotypes. In addition to using a standardized and systematic approach to ensure all candidates have equivalent chances, organizations should also invest in diversity management programs, as described in the previous section. This is valuable today, and it will become indispensable in the near future.

Concluding comments

The main objective of this book was to provide readers with an overview of the knowledge and evidence about job interviews accumulated in recent decades by psychology and management researchers. Although I tried to integrate key highlights from this line of research, this book is certainly not fully comprehensive. I encourage readers, particularly those interested in a specific sub-topic, to check the references provided in each chapter. It is also important to acknowledge that interview research is still ongoing. Every year dozens of new studies are conducted that contribute to advancing our knowledge of the psychology behind job interviews. But, of course, more research is always needed. For instance, we need to further explore the factors associated with interview success, both from the applicant's and the interviewer's perspectives, as well as how we can make interviews even more reliable, predictive of future job performance, resistant to biases, and acceptable across cultures. In other words, there is always more to be learned about the psychology of job interviews!

Notes

1 Kleinmann, M., et al., *A different look at why selection procedures work: The role of candidates' ability to identify criteria.* Organizational Psychology Review, 2011. **1**: p. 128–146.

2 Kristof-Brown, A.L., *Perceived applicant fit: Distinguishing between recruiters' perceptions of person-job and person-organization fit.* Personnel Psychology, 2000. **53**(3): p. 643–671.

3 Feeney, J.R., J.M. McCarthy, and R. Goffin, *Applicant anxiety: Examining the sex-linked anxiety coping theory in job interview contexts.* International Journal of Selection and Assessment, 2015. **23**(3): p. 295–305.

4 Bangerter, A., P. Corvalan, and C. Cavin, *Storytelling in the selection interview?: How applicants respond to past behavior questions.* Journal of Business and Psychology, 2014. **29**(4): p. 593–604.

5 Bourdage, J.S., N. Roulin, and R. Tarraf, *"I (might be) just that good": Honest and deceptive impression management in employment interviews.* Personnel Psychology, 2018, **71**(4), 597–632.

6 Robie, C., et al., *Nonlinearity in the relationship between impression management tactics and interview performance.* International Journal of Selection and Assessment, 2020. **28**(4): p. 522–530.

7 Ho, J.L., D.M. Powell, and D.J. Stanley, *The relation between deceptive impression management and employment interview ratings: A meta-analysis.* Canadian Journal of Behavioural Science/Revue canadienne des sciences du comportement, 2021. **53**(2): p. 164–174.

8 Kristof-Brown, A.L., *Perceived applicant fit: Distinguishing between recruiters' perceptions of person-job and person-organization fit.* Personnel Psychology, 2000. **53**(3): p. 643–671.

9   Latham, G.P., and D.P. Skarlicki, *The effectiveness of situational, patterned behaviour, and conventional structured interviews in minimising in-group favouritism of Canadian francophone managers.* Applied Psychology: An International Review, 1996. **45**(2): p. 177–184.

10 Levashina, J., et al., *The structured employment interview: Narrative and quantitative review of the research literature.* Personnel Psychology, 2014. **67**(1): p. 241–293.

11 Levashina, J., et al., *The structured employment interview: Narrative and quantitative review of the research literature.* Personnel Psychology, 2014. **67**(1): p. 241–293.

12 Roulin, N., A. Bangerter, and J. Levashina, *Honest and deceptive impression management in the employment interview: Can it be detected and how does it impact evaluations?* Personnel Psychology, 2015. **68**(2): p. 395–444.

13 Wilhelmy, A., et al., *How interviewers try to make favorable impressions: A qualitative study.* Journal of Applied Psychology, 2016. **101**(3): p. 313–332.

14 Lukacik, E.R., J.S. Bourdage, and N. Roulin, *Into the void: A conceptual model and research agenda for the design and use of asynchronous video interviews.* Human Resource Management Review, 2021.

15 Avery, D.R., *Support for diversity in organizations: A theoretical exploration of its origins and offshoots.* Organizational Psychology Review, 2011. **1**(3): p. 239–256.

16 Onyeador, I.N., S.-k.T.J. Hudson, and N.A. Lewis, *Moving Beyond Implicit Bias Training: Policy Insights for Increasing Organizational Diversity.* Policy Insights from the Behavioral and Brain Sciences, 2021. **8**(1): p. 19–26.

17 *Ethnic Groups in London.* 2021. https://en.wikipedia.org/wiki/Ethnic_groups_in_London;*World Population Review.* 2021. https://worldpopulationreview.com/us-cities/new-york-city-ny-population.

18 Statistics Canada/Statistique Canada. *Immigration and Ethnocultural Diversity in Canada.* 2018. https://www12.statcan.gc.ca/nhs-enm/2011/as-sa/99-010-x/99-010-x2011001-eng.cfm.

19 Lievens, F., *Research on selection in an international context: Current status and future directions*, in *Handbook of Research in International Human Resource Management*, M.M. Harris, Editor. 2007, Lawrence Erlbaum's Organizations and Management Series: New York. p. 107–123.

Index

first impression 138, 149–150, 163, 169, 179

fit 4, 57, 83, 86, 102, 104, 108, 122, 145–147, 150, 152, 156–157, 164, 168–169, 178, 180; person-job (P-J) fit 4–5, 18, 108, 145–146; person-organization (P-O) fit 5, 18, 86, 89, 104, 108, 145–146, 151–152

GDPR 135–137

halo 148, 155–156, 168–169

impression management 83–84, 87–91, 94, 97–99, 101–102, 177, 180–181, 183

inclusion 12, 120, 153, 166

job requirements 4, 9, 18, 21, 24, 77, 145, 176, 179–181

knowledge 4–5, 9–11, 18, 20, 25, 27, 29, 33, 36, 43, 57, 64, 85, 89, 102–104, 111, 162, 176, 179, 185–186

legislation 70, 73–74, 135–136, 153, 185

panel 22–23, 36, 42–43, 46, 72, 94, 107–108, 139, 154, 170–171, 184

personality 2, 5, 7, 36, 59, 66, 90–91, 96, 99, 108, 134, 144–146, 151–152, 154, 163, 176–178

preparation 10, 44, 53, 55–58, 130–133, 138–140, 177

probing 29–30, 32, 77, 94, 139–140, 179

question type: past-behavioural question 28–29, 32, 34, 36–39, 43, 94, 179; situational question 32–34, 37–38, 40, 43, 94, 179

reactions 12, 23, 25, 53, 56, 63–71, 75, 100, 121–122, 124–126, 132, 134–135, 138, 163–164, 180–181, 183

reliability 8–12, 24, 36, 42, 44, 96, 134, 138, 180

similarity 61, 86, 89, 104–105, 148, 151–154, 156, 169; similar-to-me 152, 154, 164, 168, 179–180

situation-task-action-result (STAR) 30–31, 43, 67, 76–77, 177, 179

skills 4–5, 9, 18–21, 24–28, 31, 33–35, 37–38, 41, 43–44, 54, 59–61, 67, 70, 75–77, 85–86, 89, 96, 109–110, 125, 131, 145, 170, 176–177, 179, 182

standardization 20, 43, 76, 108, 153, 179; standardized 2, 8, 11, 20–23, 29–30, 36, 53, 58, 67, 70, 94, 124, 126, 139, 150–151, 153, 158, 165, 169, 179, 180, 184–185